H2O

HEALTH 2 OVERCOME

LEO G. SZYMBORSKI IV

Preface

I didn't set out to write a book. I set out to survive.
To heal…
To understand…

Along the way, I uncovered stories, some painful, some funny, and some I thought I'd buried long ago. Yet they all had one thing in common: they shaped me into the man I am today.

This isn't just a story about water.

This is a story about the toxins we carry physically, emotionally, and generationally, and what it takes to cleanse them from ourselves. It's about growing up with the stigma of dyslexia and being told I would never make it. It's about losing people I once loved, nearly losing myself, and discovering that real healing doesn't come from a pill, it comes from having a purpose.

I've been a fighter, a father, a plumber, a bouncer, a builder, and an inventor. I've worked in toxic chemical plants and spent years learning how to remove the very poisons I once lived among. Now, I help others protect what matters most through something as simple and sacred as water.

If you've ever felt broken, doubted, dismissed, or worn down, this book is for you.

It's not polished. It's not perfect.

It's real.

Just like the road that brought me to where I am today.

Thank you for walking this path with me.

- Leo G. Szymborski

Dedication

To my wife, LeAnn

Your love didn't just support me, it *revived* me. When the world around me was falling apart, you held the pieces together. Through heartbreak, hard-won victories, and the battles in between, you stood beside me. You've seen every side of me: the warrior, the wanderer, the builder, and the broken man, yet you loved me through it all.

You never gave up on me, even when I struggled to recognize the man in the mirror. This book, this second chance at life, I owe so much of it to your love.

To my mother

The original force of nature.

You taught me to fight with integrity and to love without limits. You led with your actions and your sacrifice. In every challenge I've faced, I've carried your resilience with me. When I was young, I thought you were just my mom. Now I know you were my foundation, my moral compass, and the heroine behind every good decision I ever made.

Your strength echoes through every word in these pages.

To my children, Leo, Dean, and Nadine,

You are my life's greatest achievements, not for what I've given you, but for everything you've taught me. Each of you has shown me a different kind of strength.

Leo Jr., you made me a father. You challenged me to fight harder, to dig deeper, and in return, you gave me strength when I needed it most.

Dean, your heart and courage remind me every day why I'm so proud to be your dad. Even though you're 3,000 miles away, you are always close to my heart.

Nadine, you are my sunshine. You light up every room and remind me to keep reaching for joy, no matter the struggle. Your spirit is a daily reminder of the beauty in life.

You've each given me purpose.

You are the heartbeat behind everything I do.

To My Team

To my incredible staff, LeAnn, Nadine, and Alison. They were the ones who held down the fort in the office while our techs and I went deep into the trenches, installing systems wherever the work called. Here today, Puerto Rico tomorrow, then Texas next week; you never know where we'll be.

Thank you to Leo Jr., Jimmy, Walker, and the many other techs who have covered countless miles and endured long days and never hesitated to get their hands dirty. Your dedication, sweat, and commitment have built our mission one install at a time. I couldn't do it without all of you.

And to the true friends who stood by me, especially in dark times

You know who you are. You were there when I had nothing to offer but the truth. You saw me at my worst, believed in my comeback, and walked beside me when the road was rough. You didn't just witness my journey; *you helped me carry it.*

This is for you, too.

Acknowledgments

To the doctors and wellness experts who dared to think differently

You didn't just open your minds to new possibilities; you opened a door for people like me to walk through. You challenged convention, stood up against the tide of outdated thinking, and believed in something better. Your courage gave my mission a voice. Your support gave my work a platform. Together, we've taken something once considered fringe and turned it into a lifeline. Thank you for standing beside me when I was still proving what water could become.

To my family

You lived through it all: the long nights, the early mornings, the endless road trips, and the seasons of uncertainty when I was chasing something I could feel in my heart, but couldn't yet explain. You gave me your patience when I didn't even know how to ask for it. You gave me your strength when I was running low on mine. You believed in me before the rest of the world did.

This mission cost us time and comfort, but you never once let it cost us love. For that, I am forever grateful.

To Pete

You were there when this was nothing more than an idea scribbled on a piece of paper. You jumped in with both feet when most people would have walked away. You weren't just a business partner; you were a brother. You helped me embrace a wild, heart-driven dream and turn it into a company that now changes lives. You'll always be part of the DNA of this journey. Thank you for building something real with me.

To every client who trusted me

Your faith in me was never taken lightly. Every thank-you, every phone call, every moment where someone said, "This water changed everything." *That's* what kept me going; you believed in something bigger. You believed in *me*.

And to the seekers

The ones still searching for answers. Still navigating through the noise. Still hoping that something or someone might help them feel better, live better, and be better.

I wrote this book for you because I've been there.

Disclaimer

The information contained in this book is provided for educational and informational purposes only and is not intended as medical advice. The content is not a substitute for professional medical diagnosis, treatment, or advice from a qualified healthcare provider. Always seek the guidance of your physician or other qualified health professional with any questions you may have regarding a medical condition, the use of supplements, dietary changes, exercise programs, or any other health-related decisions.

Never disregard professional medical advice or delay in seeking it because of something you have read in this book. Reliance on any information provided herein is solely at your own risk. The author and publisher make no representations or warranties with respect to the accuracy, applicability, fitness, or completeness of the contents. The author and publisher disclaim any liability directly or indirectly arising from the use or application of any information contained in this book.

Contents

Chapter 1:
One Floor Apart

Where my story begins and his ends. A legacy passed down, a life reborn.

When you were born, your grandfather's spirit rose into you." Those were the words my mother always began with when she told the story of my birth. It was 1967 in Salem County, New Jersey, and I arrived squalling in a second-floor maternity ward while one floor directly below, my grandfather lay struggling for his final breaths. In the very hour I came into the world, he was leaving it. Just a few inches of hospital floor and concrete were all that separated my first cry from his last gasp. Life above, death below, just one floor apart.

I have imagined that scene a thousand times. The delivery room was filled with the raw cries of new life as I was born, a healthy baby boy. Downstairs, in a dim and sterile hospital room, my grandfather, Leo Szymborski, lay dying, his lungs ravaged by mesothelioma, a lung cancer he'd suffered from years of working with asbestos and chemical fumes. He was a skilled plumber, one of the first ever licensed in New Jersey (proud holder of License #002), and he had spent decades providing for his family with his bare hands and pipe wrenches. But on that day, all the strength had drained from his body. The same broad hands that once hefted heavy tools now lay limp on starched white sheets. Each breath was a battle. The hospital air was heavy with antiseptic and sorrow as machines ticked and nurses spoke in hushed tones, watching over a man who was slipping away from life.

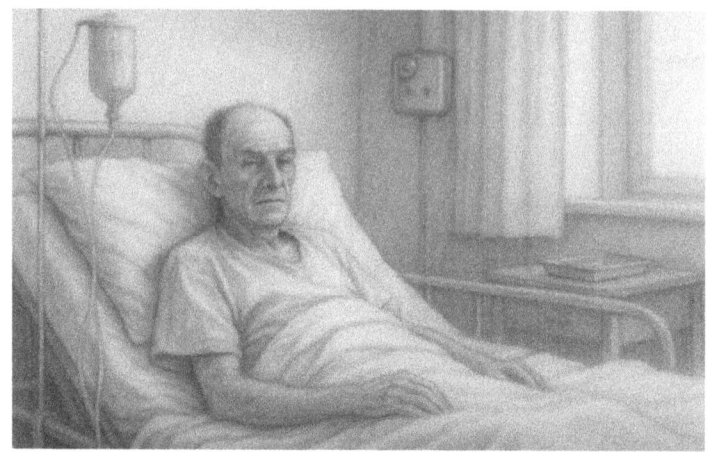

Just minutes after I was born, my father, also named Leo Szymborski, the son of the dying man and now the father of a newborn, left my mother's side in the maternity ward and rushed downstairs. His heart pounding with the clashing emotions of joy and grief. He carried the news of my birth in his heart like a fragile, precious offering. He rushed down the stairs two at a time, being too eager to wait for an elevator and determined that life's latest news should reach my grandfather, a man at the door of death, as quickly as possible.

In the hush of my grandfather's room, my father found his father pale and unconscious, the rhythmic hiss of the oxygen mask marking the seconds. Gently, he took his father's hand, a hand rough with calluses from a lifetime of manual labor, and whispered, "Dad, wake up, Dad, it's me." My grandfather's eyes fluttered open weakly, as if he sensed that something important had arrived. My father's voice trembled as he spoke the words he had been both hopeful and afraid to say: "It's a boy, Dad. You have a grandson." Pausing and swallowing hard against the lump in his throat., "He's beautiful and healthy... and we named him after you. His name is Leo."

For a moment the machines were the only sounds in the room. My grandfather's chest rose and fell with shallow motions. Then came a change: a flicker of light in his dim gaze, a final gathering of strength as he squeezed my father's hand with the faintest pressure. His lips parted, and he whispered hoarsely, his voice barely more than a breath: "Boy... boy... boy." Each word was as fragile as a soap bubble yet filled with awe. A tear slipped down my father's face as he realized his father understood. In those hoarsely whispered words, my grandfather was greeting me, celebrating me, and acknowledging the continuation of our family line with what little strength he had left.

My father leaned in, tears of joy and heartbreak mingling, and said softly, "Yes... a boy. Your grandson, Leo." A faint smile crept onto my grandfather's face. It was the last smile he ever gave. As my father watched, his dad's eyes gently closed once more, the smile still resting on his lips. The weight of that moment was enormous; having given all he could to acknowledge my birth, my grandfather drifted into a deep silence. He slipped into a coma right then, as if that brief celebration had been his final task on earth.

My grandfather never woke up again. Less than a day later, just one sunrise after my first dawn, he passed away. The nurses noted the time of death; my family noted something far more profound. In the very same hospital, one floor above, a new life had begun as his ended. He held on to life just long enough to know I had arrived. He died with the knowledge that a part of him, even if only his name, would live on.

This is how my story began: in a hospital, with laughter and tears separated by a single flight of stairs. I was born in the shadow of my grandfather's passing, forever entwined with a man I would never meet. My mother never saw it as a coincidence. She truly believed that in the exact moment he whispered "boy" and drifted into that coma, something mystical happened. "Your grandfather's spirit rose into you that day," she would tell me, her eyes shining with the intensity of that conviction. As a child, I listened wide-eyed each time she retold the tale. I grew up feeling both the weight and wonder of that legacy.

From my earliest memory, I understood that my very first act in life, being born, was tied to my grandfather's final act. I was the first grandchild, his namesake, and according to my mother, the living vessel for his departed soul. Whether or not one believes in such things, the symbolism of that moment left an indelible mark on me. I carried his name, Leo, as my own. Although it is an honor, it also felt like wearing a coat a few sizes too big, with the hope and intention that I might grow into someday. In my heart, I carried his story too, the story of a man who gave his last breath to bless my first. It made me feel special, as if I were chosen or protected, but it also made me feel deeply responsible. I was determined, even as I grew old enough to understand, that I must live a life that honored the sacrifice and struggle that came before me.

I often imagine an unseen and gentle hand guiding me, Grandpa Leo's hand steadying my shoulders whenever I felt lost. I like to think that his strength, the same strength that kept him holding on to hear of my birth, lives on in me. I have his broad shoulders and, some say, his stubbornness and smile. Perhaps that is a coincidence, or maybe it signifies something more. What I know for certain is that I have always felt a connection across time to that one hospital room below, to that final smile of his.

And that's why I've never seen my birth as a simple beginning. I wasn't just born; I was forged. Forged in the transition between generations, molded by a story of grit, love, and legacy. From the very first moment, I carried not just my name but also a mission, a purpose.

That day in 1967 was more than just the day I was born; it was the day my life became irrevocably intertwined with my grandfather's death. In the years that followed, whenever I struggled or strayed, my mother would remind me of the man whose soul might be linked to mine. "Be brave, Leo," she'd say, "Your grandfather is part of you." Those words became a source of comfort and courage. I wasn't just one life starting fresh; I was also a continuation, a living legacy.

And so my life began one floor apart from death, a beginning imbued with the echo of an ending. This profound origin taught me from the start that life and death are inseparable chapters of the same story. I learned that our lives are not only our own; we carry pieces of those who came before us. I entered the world with my grandfather's name on my birth certificate and, if my mother was right, his spirit was now in me. One life ended as another began, entangling us in a bond beyond touch or sight.

This is the foundation I was built on, and this is where my story begins.

Early Childhood – Born to Overcome

My arrival in this world was not as easy as my family had hoped. I came into life fighting, with lungs struggling to hold air and a body wracked by pneumonia and bronchitis. Those first three years of my life were a blur of illness, wheezing breaths, and high fevers, along with my mother's constant, unwavering love.

She rarely slept. Most nights, she sat beside me, her eyes red-rimmed with exhaustion yet burning with determination.

When my fever soared, sometimes reaching 106°, she would gently lift me and place me in a cool bath, whispering prayers through trembling lips. In my fevered delirium, I reached out to grasp invisible butterflies dancing along the bathroom walls, trapped in a world only I could see. Still, she never left me; her hope and love never faltered.

The hospital became my second home. The oxygen tent, both my prison and my protection, wrapped around me like a fragile cocoon. I watched the outside world through plastic, longing for the warmth of a hug. My family visited me often, their faces blurred behind the clear barrier. But one memory still shines the brightest within me: my sister Cindy, just four  years older, pressing her small hand against the plastic. I pressed mine to meet hers. It was a wordless promise: I'm still here. We're still together.

After endless nights and more hospital stays than birthdays, the doctors finally decided that my tonsils were full of infection and had to go. It was a risk, but one my mother accepted with steady resolve. And then miraculously it worked.

For the first time, I breathed without struggle.
For the first time, I wasn't "the sick child."
For the first time, I could run, laugh, and chase life instead of being chased by it.

I was born to overcome. And this was just the beginning.

Looking back, I realize that my birth wasn't just the beginning of my life; it was the continuation of something much older, much deeper. I was the next verse in a song already being sung, the next breath in a family line that never stopped pushing forward, no matter how hard the wind blew.

My grandfather's life, his strength, and even his death shaped me before I could speak. His tools may have been his bare hands and wrenches, but what he really passed down was something far more sacred: grit, pride, and the will to build a better life for those who came after him.

My earliest memories are of struggle, gasping for air, clinging to life, my mother's hands like a lighthouse beacon through the storm.

I didn't know it then, but I was already living out the legacy he left behind: to fight, to endure, and to rise.

It's strange how the most fragile beginnings can forge the strongest foundations.

I may have been born sick, yes, but I was also born surrounded by love, legacy, and purpose.

That combination became my armor. It gave me a reason to keep breathing, keep evolving, and keep moving forward.

And it reminds me, even today, that I didn't just survive. I inherited a mission and a purpose.

Chapter 2:
A Childhood Like No Other

In thirty houses, I found the whole world.

I grew up in a town so small that it felt more like a heartbeat than a place. Life moved slowly and gently. Neighbors weren't just familiar, they were family. And in that space, my childhood bloomed.

We grew up in a small neighborhood with only about 30 homes. I was the only boy my age, surrounded by a sea of girls, but I was never lonely. Cindy became my first 'buddy'. I would follow my sister everywhere, even to her friends' homes. This would have been great in my teens, but being a little boy, not so much. I knew Cindy wasn't as happy as I was. Living in our small town, having her little brother around all the time wasn't always fun for her.

I remember one time when my sister had a sleepover at her best friend's house. She was about nine, and I was five years old. Her friend's sister said I could come over, too. There were all the girls in the neighborhood, with at least ten of us in total. I told my mother I really wanted to go, but I was afraid since I had never been to a sleepover before. My mom asked why I was afraid, and I told her I was worried I would get pregnant. My mother laughed and said, "You cannot get pregnant, you're a boy, only girls can." I felt stupid, but remember, all my friends from town were girls, and I had heard them tell stories like 'If you sleep with someone, be careful, or you could get pregnant.' Well, I was sleeping over with about ten girls. I thought the odds were bad for me, and I would probably get pregnant. What does a five-year-old know anyway? Looking back, it may be the funniest thing I've ever said.

My sister was my everything; my compass, my partner in crime. I chased after her everywhere, my tiny legs pumping to keep up. She tried to lose me sometimes, craving a sliver of freedom, but I was too fast. In a town of only thirty homes, there weren't many hiding places.

We were inseparable. I couldn't imagine a world without her right beside me. Life, as it tends to do, would change that, but those memories remain: the two of us racing through the woods, scooping up frogs and turtles from sparkling brooks, building forts and dreaming of castles.

And one day, we found one. One of the most amazing places in town was a grand old house tucked away behind the other properties, owned by the Summers family. To my young eyes, it seemed nothing short of a castle. With its sprawling grounds and carefully tended gardens, it felt like a hidden paradise. My sister was friends with one of the granddaughters, which meant I got a golden ticket to step inside this incredible home a few times. I remember standing in awe, overwhelmed by its size and elegance. It was the biggest house I had ever seen.

But even in fairytales, there is sorrow. Mrs. Summers, the lady of the house, was bedridden, confined to a single room, while the beauty of her land passed her by. Yet her granddaughters knew its magic, and through them, so did we.

Years later, the house changed hands. A doctor moved in. I returned not as a boy chasing adventure, but as a man hired to install a water filtration system. The grandeur had faded. The house felt smaller, or maybe I had grown. Still, for a brief moment, I stood still and remembered a childhood that overflowed with joyful memories of that house.

Halloween meant hayrides, thanks to our neighbor Jimmy Luciano, who became a lifelong friend. Jimmy would ride his dad's tractor and would pull us through the crisp October air, across a little brick bridge we called "poosticks," built by his father. We crossed those brooks for fun, not knowing they would later become part of our story.

My parents, young and hopeful, did their best to hide the hardships from us. Money was tight, but we never felt it. My mother was a magician, spinning joy from scarcity. She'd blast '60s music as she cleaned, twirling and laughing as if we lived in a dream.

Some nights, we had pancakes for dinner. Yet she made it all feel like a game, a grand adventure. I never realized it was out of necessity. I never noticed the quiet sacrifices. But now, I see what I didn't see then.

And I wouldn't trade that small-town childhood for anything in the world.

A Childhood in the Shadow of a Chemical Plant

My sister and I always knew what kind of day our father had at the chemical plant by the way he smelled. The chemicals clung to him, sinking into his skin and clothes. It was a scent we associated with love, strength, and home. We had no idea how dangerous it was. It was just Dad.

Years later, I still carried the same burden. Coming home from work, coated in the same toxic remnants, I understood. My wife would stop me at the door, insisting I strip down in the stairwell before coming inside. I understood then what my father had unknowingly brought home: the poison of an honest day's labor.

From age two to nine, we lived just a mile from that chemical plant. A quiet, unassuming town. But beneath the calm, something dark seeped into our lives. A canal ran nearby, tainted by the plant's runoff. Our wells drew from that earth. We drank it. We bathed in it. We lived in it.

And we paid the price.

Everyone I knew from that time, those who are still alive, has lost most or all of their teeth. The water was poisoned. It stole our health quietly over the years. We didn't know. But other towns knew and they drew water from faraway sources. They stayed safe.

When my mother was expecting my little brother, Steven, we needed more space. This was when we moved to a new town.

This new town was livelier, bustling with kids and possibilities. I had new friends, a space, and a fresh start. But what I loved the most? The Wawa down the street.

If you don't know Wawa, you've missed out. Back then, it had a deli. And for a boy with a few coins in his pocket, it was heaven. I went for hot chocolate, for sticky buns, for something sweet in a world that didn't always feel that way.

Still, the pull of my first town never faded.

Fifteen miles might not seem far, but to a boy on a bike, it was an odyssey. I pedaled back whenever I could. The neighbors would spot me and call my mom. She always knew. At dinner, she'd say with a smile, "I heard you've been exploring again."

That was all she needed to say.

Sister Cindy and Me

She never scolded me. I think she knew my soul was born restless, wired for wonder. She let me chase it. She let me be me.

And now, all these years later, I'd give anything to go back just for one day...

...To that little town... to that house... to my family, whole and laughing... to my father, walking in from work, still smelling of sacrifice... to my sister's laughter echoing through the trees... to the boy I once was, running wild in a world that felt endless.

What I wouldn't give to return home one more time to where it all started!

Time has a way of sweetening memory, even when it's laced with things we didn't understand. I look back on that little town and feel nothing but warmth, even as I now know what lingered beneath the surface, what crept into our water, our lungs, our bones.

As kids, we didn't see the danger. We saw frogs in brooks, forts in the woods, and magic in old houses. We smelled our father's work and called it love. We drank the water and called it life.

It's only now, as a man, that I understand what we were up against and what my parents never told us they feared. And even now, knowing the cost, I wouldn't trade it. Because that town, that time, shaped me. It filled me with wonder. It gave me a fighting spirit.

Maybe that's what childhood is: not realizing what's broken until you're old enough to fix it.

And maybe that's why I do what I do now. I drank from poisoned wells and lived to survive. But I don't want the next child just to survive, I want them to thrive.

And it all started there in that small town of thirty homes, where everything began.

Chapter 3:
The Shift

Violence can shatter childhood innocence, but it can also forge a protector.

The Inspiration Behind the Strength

The inspiration behind my love for martial arts and weight training runs far deeper than a simple passion for physical strength. It is rooted in a defining moment from my childhood, an event so traumatic that it changed the course of my life forever.

To understand my drive to protect, my need to lead, and even my response to certain smells and situations, I need to share a horror that no child should ever have to witness.

A Day That Changed Everything

Between the ages of seven and nine, I attended St. James Catholic Grammar School in Penns Grove, New Jersey. The air in our school was always thick with the scent of primordial incense from the church, a fragrance that should have evoked peace, but for me, it will always be linked to terror.

On the morning of February 24, 1975, at exactly 9:10 AM, an intruder walked into my second-grade classroom. There were twenty-four of us innocent children, barely seven years old, sitting at our desks.

"Good morning, class," the man said.

Our teacher, Miss Kate Flynn, just 25 years old, looked up, startled. She began to ask if she could help him when, suddenly, he raised a 12-gauge shotgun and fired.

The deafening blast filled the room. Blood splattered across the walls.

Miss Flynn screamed in agony, the first shot tearing into her arm, the second into her abdomen. Shotguns don't just wound, they destroy. The horror on her face was unbearable. But even in excruciating pain, she fought to protect us.

"Get down! Hide!" she yelled.

I froze. My ears rang. My classmates screamed in terror as bullets whizzed through the air. Some of my classmates dove into the coat closet, burying themselves under jackets, too young to comprehend what was happening. I half-crawled, half-ran toward the hallway, my small body trembling with fear.

The chaos was overwhelming; the sound of gunfire, the cries of children, the desperate screams of teachers. Just as I reached the door, our priest, who was also the school's principal, rushed toward the classroom. He was only 38 years old, but he didn't hesitate.

He confronted the shooter, trying to stop him.

I turned just in time to see the gunman shoot him in the head. I was certain I was next.

But as the shooter fled down the fire escape, I somehow found my way to another classroom. The teachers shouted out the windows for someone to call the police. Back then, there were no cell phones or any way to instantly notify parents. We were left in fear, waiting for the nightmare to end.

Eventually, we were put on a bus and sent home. When I arrived, my mother was waiting for me. She pulled me into her arms, whispering words of comfort. I sat on the couch, feeling numb, still smelling the gunpowder on my clothes.

The shooter was later caught running along the Delaware River. He had once been an All-American athlete with a bright future. But mental illness and drug abuse had taken over his life.

Living with the Trauma

In the 1970s, there was no trauma counseling for us children. No one understood the long-term effects of witnessing such violence. We were given a short break from school and then thrown back into the very same classrooms where blood had been spilled.

I struggled. The trauma mixed with my undiagnosed dyslexia made learning nearly impossible. The words on the page seemed to crawl like ants, refusing to form sentences. I felt lost and disconnected.

The year after the shooting, I begged my parents to take me out of Catholic school. My mother, seeing my suffering, agreed. I transferred to a public grammar school in our new town. It felt like a fresh start.

I made friends, including Rob, a classmate who would later become one of my closest companions. However, the trauma never truly left me.

Trauma doesn't disappear. It lingers and shapes who we become.

A Flashback That Sent Me Running

One morning in fourth grade, I sat at my desk, finally feeling some sense of normalcy. Suddenly, I heard gunshots.

They came from the woods nearby, where hunters fired at a deer. But to me, in my traumatized child's mind, it was February 24, 1975, all over again.

Without thinking, I bolted. I ran two miles straight home, adrenaline pumping through my veins. When I arrived, my mother was already waiting for me at the front door as the school had called her to let her know what had happened.

That day, it was decided that I would be homeschooled for several months before transferring to a specialized school that could help me with both my trauma and my learning challenges.

There, at that new school, for the first time, I had a teacher who understood me. She introduced me to a simple yellow transparency sheet, something that miraculously allowed me to read. The words finally stopped moving around like ants on the page. For the first time, I felt hopeful.

From Survivor to Protector

Though I didn't know it at the time, that horrifying day in my second-grade classroom set me on a path toward strength, discipline, and protection.

I never wanted to feel powerless again.

I soon immersed myself in martial arts and weight training, not just to build my body, but to strengthen my mind. I became a leader, someone others could rely on, because I understood what it meant to be afraid.

To this day, the primordial smell of incense brings back everything I experienced on that fateful day. It sends a chill down my spine, a visceral reaction so strong that I have to leave the room. Weddings, funerals, church services, if incense is burned, I have to walk away.

Trauma doesn't disappear. It lingers, shaping who we become.

I know how deeply school shootings scar the soul. I still carry that day in my bones; every loud bang, every whiff of incense or gunpowder pulls me right back to that classroom.

My heart breaks for the kids who endure what I did. That kind of trauma never truly leaves you.

That day planted something in me. It wasn't fear, but purpose. I didn't just want strength, I wanted to be ready. I trained so I could act when others froze, so I'd never feel powerless again.

Pain may shape us, but it doesn't define us.

Change crept in quietly after we left that little town, away from poisoned water and childhood dreams. A shift began. In my family. In how I saw the world. In how I saw myself.

I started asking hard questions: Why do some people carry so much pain? Why do some families never seem to catch a break?

And deep down, I began to feel that maybe everything I had experienced, everything I'd survived, wasn't random.

It was a map, an opportunity.

And soon, it would lead me somewhere I never expected.

Chapter 4:
Big Brother, Bigger Lessons

When my little brother Steven was born, everything changed, even if I didn't realize it right away.

My Brother Steven

At just ten years old, I found myself navigating a whirlwind of change. We had moved to a new town and I was adapting to a new school. But best of all, there was a new addition to our family: my baby brother, Steven.

His arrival brought a kind of joy I hadn't expected. He became the bright spark of our household, and I embraced my role as big brother with enthusiasm. I adored playing with him. On trips to the store, I'd plop Steven in a cart and race down the aisles, imitating the roar of an engine as his laughter echoed like music.

In many ways, he mirrored my own childhood. Just as I had followed my older sister Cindy everywhere, now Steven tagged along after me. For the first five years of his life, Steven was my little shadow. We had endless adventures, and I loved having someone to share my energy with.

But things change.

By the time he turned five, I was fifteen, wrapped up in karate, weightlifting, and work. The ten-year gap between us grew wider. I didn't mean to drift away from him, but I did. Life pulled me in a different direction, and I didn't always notice how much he still looked up to me.

One moment, though, has never left me.

Like many brothers, we often played rough. One day, I went too far, nothing serious, but enough that Steven started to cry. I panicked, thinking I'd get in trouble, and began offering him toys or snacks to calm him down.

But Steven didn't want toys. He didn't want anything.

Through his tears, he looked up at me and said, "I don't need anything from you. I just want to play with you."

He didn't want a bribe. He wanted me, his big brother.

That moment opened my eyes. I realized how much he still needed me, and how much I had taken our bond for granted. From that day on, I tried to show up for him in a different way, not just as someone fun to follow around, but as someone who led with love and presence.

Childhood Influences and the Paths They Shape

While Steven brought a new emotional dimension to my life, I was also being shaped by the deep, hands-on lessons passed down through generations.

My roots run deep as a third-generation plumber. The legacy started with my grandfather, whose New Jersey plumbing license was #002, only the second license in the entire state. He wasn't just a master of his trade; he was a trailblazer, a visionary who built a steadfast future with his hands, long before the word "entrepreneur" became a buzzword.

But the environment he worked in was brutal. Chemical plants. Toxic air. Dangerous substances like cyanide and tetraethyllead. The stories I heard as a kid were chilling, such as the one of this man who stood by a toxic wastewater stream, fishing with no line, his mind lost to the chemicals surrounding him.

Cancer was everywhere in Salem County, New Jersey. It became known by the locals as a "cancer cluster." Everyone was connected to someone affected by these dangerous, toxic chemicals.

And eventually, I too, felt the pain of someone becoming affected.

Over the years, my father and I found ourselves working in those same hazardous environments, places soaked in chemical fumes and blanketed with asbestos dust. The walls, the ceilings, and even the very air we breathed felt contaminated. We lost the father of my childhood friend Rob to cancer, a slow and brutal disease likely born from years of exposure in those toxic surroundings. Years later, Rob's mother also passed away from cancer. She had worked around harsh industrial chemicals for decades and I have no doubt that the contamination from the chemicals played a part in stealing her life as well.

Even as a kid, I was learning about sacrifice, exposure, and resilience.

But my childhood wasn't defined solely by danger. It was filled with moments that sparked passion and pride.

My dad brought me along on countless projects, teaching me the ropes. One day, he brought home discarded gas-powered water pumps, which might be junk to someone but were a treasure to me. I was around eleven or twelve and determined to make something out of nothing.

Without any YouTube or internet tutorials, I tinkered with parts until I finally got one working. That engine became the heart of my first minibike. I'll never forget the look on my dad's face when he saw me zipping around the yard, using my sneakers as brakes.

My mechanical roots run deep on both sides of the family. My Pop Pop, my mom's father, was a mechanic who owned a gas station and repair shop. Later, he ran a small engine business from home. Weekends spent in his garage felt like stepping into a live classroom. I watched my Pop Pop and uncle work on lawnmower engines, mesmerized, absorbing everything.

Pop Pop had a soft spot for teasing me. He'd tugged at my long hair and joked about needing a haircut; it was the '70s, after all. Long hair was in, and I wore it like a badge of honor.

Still, school was always a struggle. While I could take apart an engine and put it back together without blinking, reading a book felt like trying to decode a foreign language. My brain wouldn't focus. It was as if someone had built a wall between me and the words.

I saw this as a curse, something that left me feeling broken in the classroom even as I thrived in the garage.

But life has a way of giving us what we need, even when it doesn't make sense at the time. I may not have been able to focus on a textbook, but I could focus on real-world problems. I could build. I could repair. I could create.

Those lessons stuck with me.

They became part of who I was.

They were teaching me something school never could. And looking back now, I can see it clearly:

All of it was preparing me not just to build a life. It was preparing me to help others.

Chapter 5:
Forged in Fire: My Teenage Years

From trauma to training, my discipline turned me from a scared kid into a warrior in the making.

Adolescence hit me like a wave: part freedom, part confusion, part fire in my chest that I couldn't quite explain. By the time I was a teenager, the world felt like it was cracking open with opportunity and pressure all at once. I was eager to grow up, to explore, to figure out who I was beyond the shadows of childhood trauma and the roles I had played at home.

Cars became an obsession. There was something about the hum of an engine, the smell of grease, the thrill of fixing something with my own hands and intuition; it all combined to give me purpose. While some of my friends talked about sports or hunting, I found my rhythm in the garage, piecing together engines, turning up old beaters (cars), and dreaming of the day I could build something entirely on my own.

But being a teenager wasn't all horsepower and oil. I still struggled in school, constantly at odds with textbooks and tests. I knew I wasn't dumb; I could figure out any machine you put in front of me, but the classroom made me feel broken. Teachers didn't always understand kids like me, the ones who learned with their hands and their hearts, not just their eyes.

Still, I found ways to thrive. Martial arts gave me discipline. The gym gave me strength. Working with my dad, whether plumbing a new system or tackling weekend jobs, gave me skills no classroom ever could. I started to feel the pull of independence. I wanted to earn my own money, buy my own tools, and someday, maybe even start my own business.

But those years weren't just about work; they were about friendship too. Late-night drives with Rob and the crew, music blaring, windows down. Summer nights by the river.

First crushes, awkward dances, getting into a little trouble, and figuring out where the line was before I crossed it.

My teenage years were messy and full of lessons. They weren't perfect, but they belonged to me. Gradually, without even realizing it, I was building something much bigger than a minibike or my muscles. I was building myself.

Weight Training: The Brotherhood of Strength

Rob and I started weight training when we were just thirteen. His mom's garage became our first gym. It was equipped with a bench, some free weights, and a tiny kerosene heater that barely warmed the air during the dead of winter. Some days, we had no heat at all. But we trained anyway. Pain, cold, exhaustion; nothing stopped us.

By the age of fourteen, we joined a real gym, ironically called "The Gym," and Rob still has a picture of us standing outside on the day we joined. We were both so skinny. At 6 ft. tall and just 155 pounds, I looked like a stick. But with years of hard work, I eventually bulked up to 180 pounds, still lean, but now packed with strength.

When Rob was sixteen, he entered the Mr. Eastern Seaboard bodybuilding competition at the YMCA. One of his competitors turned out to be my cousin, whom I hadn't seen in years. I helped Rob prepare backstage doing towel pulls for resistance training, and then watched with pride as he stepped onto the stage. He nailed his routine and took first place, beating everyone, including my cousin. It was a huge moment for him and for me as his training partner.

Martial Arts and the Will to Protect

At the same time, martial arts became equally important to me. I was still haunted by the memory of the school shooting I had survived as a child. On some subconscious level, it fueled my desire to be strong. Not just physically, but mentally. I wanted to protect myself, yes, but I also wanted to protect others.

Growing up, Steve was into Karate, Rob was into bodybuilding, and I was caught between both worlds. Rob and I trained hard. I joined Steve at the dojo, the hall in which to practice martial arts, and soon, I found myself doing both Karate on Tuesdays, Thursdays, and Saturdays, as well as weightlifting on the other days.

And I didn't just train, I pushed myself to extremes.

One of the most brutal parts of Karate was the Kiba-Dachi, or horse stance. It sounds simple: feet shoulder-width apart and knees bent low, but our instructor made us hold that stance for an entire 90-minute class. My legs would tremble. My back would ache, and when I started to falter, the instructor would walk by and kick the backs of my knees to test me.

If I dropped, I had to get back up.

I would rather have fought the toughest guy in the class than hold that position for an hour and a half. But it forged something deep in me: discipline, focus, and mental toughness. It wasn't about being the best, it was about refusing to quit.

The Conflict: Strength vs. Agility

As I got deeper into both worlds, I started hearing conflicting advice. My Karate instructors said I was building too much muscle, which was limiting my flexibility. My weightlifting friends warned that Karate was holding me back from reaching my full bodybuilding potential.

They were both right.

But I wasn't willing to give up either. I didn't want to be just a fighter. Or just a lifter. I wanted to be strong, balanced, and capable of defending myself in any situation.

I wasn't the best martial artist, and I wasn't the best bodybuilder, but I was becoming something greater: someone who could endure.

The Price of Pushing Too Hard

Looking back, I pushed my body past its limits more times than I can count. There were mornings when I could barely walk and days when my legs were so sore after squats that I had to stretch just to stand up straight. And driving my hot rod with its heavy clutch after a 'leg day' was a nightmare. I'd have to time every shift perfectly just to avoid using the clutch so I would not stall out.

My biggest fear was having to hold Kiba-Dachi after one of those grueling leg days.

Luckily for me, that horror never materialized.

Reclaiming Power

Looking back, I see it so clearly now.

Martial arts and weight training weren't just physical outlets. They were in therapy. They were the disciplines that made me feel in control in a world that once felt chaotic. They were the foundation of the man I was becoming.

The little boy who once cowered in fear during a school shooting grew into someone who could stand his ground. The child who once ran became the young man people could rely on.

I wasn't just surviving anymore; I was becoming.

The horrors of my past didn't define me. They forged me. And even now, all these years later, that fire still burns.

Popcorn, Paychecks, and Teenage Chaos— Movie Theater Fun! (My First Real Job)

When I was 15, my friends and I decided to sneak into a horror movie at the local theater. It was rated R, and we needed to be 17, but we were big guys, tall and broad, and figured we could pass. That plan fell apart when we walked in and ran straight into Mr. Cable, the theater manager.

Only, Mr. Cable wasn't just any manager; he was my old neighbor from our small hometown. I remembered him well.

He was a car guy who collected old Cadillacs, and I'd always admired his collection. When he recognized me, I thought I was busted. He looked me over and asked, "How old are you, son?"

Panic kicked in. I didn't want to lie, but I definitely didn't want to say I was only 15. So, I blurted out, "Sixteen," hoping that would do the trick.

To my surprise, he didn't lecture me or throw me out. Instead, he smiled and said, "Perfect. I'm looking for a new door guy. You're hired."

And just like that, I went from sneaking into movies to working in the theater. It would become the best job I'd ever had. Free movies. Cool people. A paycheck. I was all in.

One of the first people I became close to was Jim, a senior in high school who worked as an usher. We hit it off immediately. On our days off, we'd head to the Delaware Theater at Christiana Mall to watch new releases. My mom used to joke, "You work at a movie theater and still go watch more movies," But we couldn't help it. We were hooked.

Eventually, Jim found out I wasn't really 16, but that I was a freshman who had been held back in third grade. I was embarrassed at first, but Jim didn't care. He saw me for who I was, not how old I was. He became like an older brother to me. He even taught me how to tie a tie, a skill no one in my plumber-heavy family had ever needed to show me. When he got married, he asked me to be his best man. That meant the world to me.

And then there was Mr. Cable. One night, as I was mopping up spilled soda and popcorn, he came over and said, "This is going to be the best job you've ever had."

At the time, I wasn't so sure. But he was right.

There were the classic theater moments with syrup all over the soda machine, crawling up to the big outdoor marquee every Thursday night to change the movie titles. I was a terrible speller, so I'd mess it up and become the laughingstock of the school. I didn't last long in that role, but I never stopped enjoying the work.

It was at that job where I met my first girlfriend. I learned how to talk to people, how to joke around, and how to handle conversations with people from all walks of life. I wasn't just the quiet kid with a hard past anymore; I was becoming someone people liked being around. Someone who could connect.

Mr. Cable was right. It was the best job I ever had.

And during that time, as my confidence grew, so did my passion for cars. I was already into fitness and martial arts, but now I was also diving into muscle car rebuilds. It all came together: training my body, tuning engines, working hard, and chasing that feeling of bringing something broken back to life.

Looking back, those movie theater nights were just as important as the days spent in the dojo or the garage. The job, the work, the training all showed me how to be myself, not just strong, but real. Not just disciplined, but engaged.

Every bag of popcorn, every awkward date, and every late-night cleanup shaped me just as much as Karate or weightlifting did.

This gave me more than I realized at the time.

This gave me a reason to keep going.

And most of all, this showed me something I'd forgotten: Pain might build strength, but joy... joy builds connection. And that's what I needed most.

Chapter 6:
Grit, Grease, and Guts

Building my first car taught me more than any classroom ever could.

While other kids were saving up for sneakers or stereos, I had one goal: to build my own car. Not to buy one, but build it from scratch.

I didn't want a hand-me-down or a beat-up ride from a lot. I wanted something I could build from the ground up. Something that was mine, bolt by bolt. I wanted to understand how every part worked and how it all came together... or didn't.

That car became my obsession, my classroom, my rebellion, and my escape.

Muscle Cars

By the time I turned 16, I had already built my first car, a 1974 Dodge Dart Sport Hang 10. I spent months in our home garage working on that car through scorching summer heat and freezing winter cold, doing whatever it took to get it running smoothly. I didn't know much about engines at the time, but I had an innate mechanical understanding that helped me get through it. Technical manuals became my bible, and I wasn't afraid to ask the local experts for advice.

The result? A car that purred like a tiger, that was alive and ready to roar.

My dad stepped in to help me rebuild the engine, and by New Year's Eve, just a few months before I turned 17, we were finished. I bought the car from my cousin for $50 and spent around $500 (the equivalent of approximately $4,000 today) on the rebuild. It was my pride and joy, and I couldn't wait to take it for a spin.

And here's where things get interesting.

On New Year's Eve, my parents went out to celebrate, leaving my friend Rob and I at home to babysit my little brother, Steven, who was only six at the time. With the clock ticking down to midnight, I thought, "Why not take the car out for a spin to ring in the New Year?

So Rob, Steven, and I piled into the Dodge and took the back road behind our house.

Here's the deal: my car had open headers, meaning it was loud. Like, dragster loud. It was basically our fireworks for the night. I hadn't installed the exhaust system yet, so as we sped down the road, people popped their heads out of their homes to see what in the world was making all that noise at midnight.

It was a thrilling ride, and somehow, we dodged the cops. Lucky for me, because if they had caught us, I would've been in serious trouble.

That was just the beginning.

Over the next few years, Rob and I tore up the streets and racetracks in the muscle cars I built. Rob called me "Motor Head," and I called him "Muscle Head." It was a perfect fit.

While our friends were out partying with beer in hand, we were on a mission to get bigger, stronger, and faster. Our "drink of choice" was milk, and our diet was intense; we ate like animals. One time, we had a contest to see who could gain the most weight in 30 days.

I stuffed my face with anything I could find: large pizzas, cheesesteaks, whatever I could get my hands on. My mom nearly kicked me out of the house because of all the food I was devouring. But after 30 days, we each only gained about 2 or 3 pounds. Looking back, I'm not even sure who won. All I know is... I miss that metabolism.

The Birth of a Business Mind

By my late teens, I had built and sold quite a few muscle cars, mostly in the late '60s and early '70s classics. I wish I had kept some of those cars as they'd be worth a fortune now.

But I wasn't thinking about value back then. I was thinking about the next build. I had become so skilled at working on cars that people from all over, friends, family, neighbors, started bringing me their cars for everything from brake jobs to full-on engine rebuilds.

Soon, our yard resembled a used car dealership or a muscle car museum in progress. My mom wasn't thrilled with the constant parade of vehicles, but she didn't stop me. She saw how much I loved it. She didn't want to crush that passion, so she let me pursue it.

That's when I realized I didn't just have a passion for cars. I had the instincts of an entrepreneur.

More Than Machines

The more I worked on engines, the more I learned about myself. It wasn't just about fixing cars; it was about building a life. Every car I brought back to life felt like proof that I could do something that mattered. That I had a future.

By my twenties, I was all in. No longer just fixing things, rather I was creating, all from the ground up.

Word spread around the town. People started talking about my work. If someone's car broke down or if they wanted to upgrade their ride, they came to me. My garage had become a mini auto shop, and soon enough, it was overflowing. Some cars barely ran, while others were fresh off the lot and waiting for an upgrade.

It was organized chaos. And I loved it.

The Empire Under Construction

I wasn't just a car enthusiast.

I was a businessman in the making.

Every project felt personal. Every car was a challenge. A canvas. I poured everything into each one. The smell of grease and the sound of tools clanking on concrete were music to my ears.

I had the drive.
I had the vision.
I had the grit.

I could transform a rusty shell and turn it into a street-pounding machine.

And the thrill of hearing that first engine roar to life after hours of work, that feeling never gets old.

But it wasn't just the machines; it was the people, the shop talk, the problem-solving, and the trust people placed in me. I didn't just fix cars. I built relationships. I built a reputation. I built confidence.

I was proving something not only to the world, but also to myself.

I wasn't waiting for the opportunity. I was building it.

And the best part, I was just getting started.

School Was a Battlefield

While I was building muscle cars and confidence outside of school, inside those classroom walls, I felt like I was losing a different kind of battle.

It wasn't just about the lessons; it was about survival. My learning disability made everything feel like an uphill climb. And the teachers, most of them, didn't get it. They gave up on me. To them, I was a lost cause. And that felt like a punch in the gut every single day.

They would even read test scores out loud: "Leo… fail." Thumbs down.

It was like a game show, like I wasn't a person.

And the kids laughed.

I wanted to disappear. But by then, I had been lifting weights like a man on a mission. I had karate training. And even though it wasn't in my nature to  hurt anyone, I wasn't about to let people keep stomping on me. I stood my ground, and yeah, I got into a few brawls. After that, the bullying stopped.

The teachers didn't let up, though. They acted more like drill sergeants than mentors, trying to weed out the weak. But I wasn't weak. I just learned differently.

Even my mom struggled to understand. She thought I was just lazy, but my dad knew. He'd been there, too, dyslexic just like me. So was his father. They both dropped out of school and found their success in hard work with their hands.

And I was heading down the same road.

My last year of school felt like a warzone. Mom would beg Dad to work me so hard he'd send me running back to school. But it didn't work. Hard work was still easier than school.

So, like my father and grandfather before me, I dropped out.

But years later, my mom told me something I'll never forget. She said, "You know what your dad told me after you left school?"

I shook my head.

He said, "That boy's going to make you proud someday." That hit me right in the chest in a good way.

A New Way to See It

For those who don't know, dyslexia is a learning disability that messes with how you read, write, spell, and even how you speak sometimes. It doesn't mean you're not smart. In fact, a lot of people who are dyslexic work twice as hard just to keep up.

It's frustrating as hell.

After the shooting at my school, I wanted to serve and protect by becoming a police officer, but I knew early on that I could never be a cop, not because I didn't want to protect and serve, but because the mountain of paperwork would've crushed me. That kind of job required reading and writing skills I simply didn't have.

But here's the wild part:

Dyslexia doesn't make you stupid. It's a superpower.

Yeah, I said it.

I started seeing it for what it really was: my secret weapon. It forced me to think outside the box. It made me approach problems from angles other people missed. People with dyslexia often perceive the world in 3D or even 4D. We don't just read a letter, we see it from every side. That's why we sometimes reverse letters or numbers. But it's also why we're natural problem solvers, creators, and builders.

Many successful innovators, including Richard Branson, Steven Spielberg, and IKEA founder Ingvar Kamprad, have been open about living with dyslexia. While figures like Einstein and Edison are sometimes rumored to have had learning differences, the evidence is unclear. What is clear, however, is that people with dyslexia often develop creative problem-solving skills, resilience, and unique perspectives that can fuel innovation. We think differently. We see differently.

And that's what made me.

Legacy in the Letters

I wasn't alone in this battle. It shaped me. It forged me. And I wouldn't give it up for anything.

Back in the day, I used to send pages to my friends, you know, those old beepers from the '80s. I'd mess up the numbers every time, turning it into a game of "guess who's calling."

The struggle was real.

If I had the tools my kids have today, like spell check and voice-to-text, I know I could've finished school. But in some ways, maybe I graduated in a different way. Through life. Through hustle. Through the heart.

And here's the part that matters most to me:

LEO JR GRADUATION 3 LEOS

My first son, Leo Jr., the fifth Leo in our family line, is also dyslexic. But this time, we had the knowledge, tools, and support to help him through it. He made it.

He graduated from high school.

He is the first Leo in five generations to earn that diploma. It took five Leos to break the cycle.

And when he walked across that stage, we celebrated like he'd just graduated from Harvard. Good Job, Leo!

Hidden in Plain Sight

I discovered something I never knew about my own name, and it all began by accident.

My great-grandfather was also named Leo, the very first of us all. I didn't know much about him growing up, only that everyone called him "Lue." We all thought that was his real name. Turns out, it wasn't.

He worked as a machinist at Weston House in Philadelphia, and although he couldn't read or write, he possessed an incredible gift. He could machine parts down to ten-thousandths of an inch. That kind of precision takes real talent, especially without formal education.

I was working in Clementon, New Jersey. I had to pull over to read a map; this was before GPS, and the quietest place I could find was a nearby cemetery. I figured it would be peaceful and traffic-free, the perfect place to regroup.

As I was scanning the map, something caught my eye. I looked up and saw a headstone with my last name on it: SZYMBORSKI.

Curious, I got out of the van and walked over to the grave. It was my Uncle Charlie. I didn't even remember ever being at that cemetery before. I asked an older woman who worked there if there were any other Szymborskis buried nearby. She took me into the small office and pulled out an old, crumbling record book-no computers back then, at least not in that place.

Flipping through the pages, she found the name: Leo G. Szymborski. My great-grandfather.

It hit me like a bolt of lightning. That made me Leo IV, and I would have never known it if I hadn't pulled into that cemetery that day. Just a random stop, but one that connected me even deeper to the legacy I carried.

From Pistons to Pipes

By the time I turned 17, I was done with school. No more textbooks. No more classrooms. No more trying to squeeze my brain into something that didn't fit.

I come from a long line of stubborn, hard-headed plumbers from New Jersey, but hard-headed in the best possible way. Plumbing wasn't just a job; it was a tradition. As a third-

generation plumber, I dove straight into full-time work with my dad, carrying on the Szymborski legacy.

Like my dad and grandfather before me, I became a plumber.

My relationship with my father wasn't the "go play catch" kind. We didn't bond over sports or games; we bonded through work. He was the teacher, I was the student, learning the trade and learning about life.

Some of my best memories come from those long days working side by side, even though it wasn't always smooth sailing. My dad didn't give out compliments. He was blunt. Tough. Classic Jersey.

One day, I made a mistake on a job that cost him money. His response:

"Boy, I wish I had your brains."

I asked, "Why?"

He smirked and said, "Because they're brand new. You've never used them."

The whole crew cracked up. But for me, it stung. It wasn't just a jab; it was a lesson. And I made damn sure I never made that mistake again.

Years later, I told that story at my dad's funeral. When I did, the whole room erupted in laughter because they all knew. That was just him; that was his way.

Most of our work was in South Jersey, where homes relied on well water. However, that water was contaminated with acid rain from nearby chemical plants, corroding the copper plumbing. Pinholes, blue-green stains, and leaks were everywhere around the town.

It was a nightmare, but it also lit a fire within me.

My dad saw how I naturally gravitated toward problem-solving. Whenever we hit a wall, he'd say, "Alright, Boy Genius. Go figure this out." So, I did.

I took a water treatment course in Philly. I learned about pH levels, corrosion, and what others were doing to fix the problem. Many plumbers added crushed marble to neutralize the acid, and city systems used lye or bicarbonates to treat water. We tried acid neutralizers, too, but it quickly became clear they weren't enough. The pH only reached 6.0, which was still too acidic.

But I wasn't done yet. I had to solve this problem.

I started experimenting with minerals, magnesium oxide, and other alkaline materials. That did the trick. We adjusted the pH to a neutral range of 7.0 to 7.5. The problem was finally resolved.

Or so we thought.

With acid neutralizers, a new issue of hard water arose; lime scale and water spots appeared everywhere. So we added water softeners. That fixed the hardness, but now the sodium levels were too high and not good for people with heart conditions.

Back to the drawing board.

That's when I helped develop a tri-phase solution:

1. Acid neutralizer to fix the pH

2. Water softener to manage mineral content

3. Reverse osmosis system to remove the salt for clean drinking water

It worked. We finally had a system that solved every layer of the problem. It was a game-changer.

Through it all, every challenge, every failure, every breakthrough, my parents kept encouraging me. They reminded me repeatedly that I could do anything I set my mind to.

Even with my struggles in school, they believed in me.

They taught me that success doesn't come from perfect grades. It comes from showing up, working hard, and never quitting.

And that's exactly what I did.

I never imagined I'd progress beyond being a tradesman. I didn't think I was cut out to run a business. I didn't know the language, and I had no formal training. But I had a sharp instinct for numbers. I had the hustle and the grit needed to flourish.

And I learned everything quickly. If I didn't know something, I'd put myself around people who did.

That's how, at 20 years old, I took the leap.

I got myself into the water purification business.

But I knew deep down...

I will say it again, this was only the beginning.

Lessons in the Dojo: When the Student becomes the Teacher

One evening, I was teaching a beginner karate class at the dojo when a man walked in. He looked nervous and unsure, like he didn't belong there, but something in his eyes felt familiar. As we started training, I noticed how uncomfortable he was, how unsure. He mentioned that he'd been getting bullied. I didn't ask by whom.

But then I looked again. Really looked.

And it hit me like a punch to the gut-it was my old math teacher.

The one who made my life miserable.

The one who humiliated me in front of the class. The one who made me feel like I was stupid.

Now he was in my class.

A wave of anger surged through me. I remembered every public "F" he called out in the classroom, every time he made me feel small. But I didn't lash out-not right away. I kept my cool... mostly. I still threw a few heavy punches during drills, just enough to show him who was in control this time.

After class, my instructor pulled me aside. "What was that all about?" he asked.

I shrugged. "Some old payback," I said, half-smirking. He gave me that look-the kind that said, "Don't do it again." And I didn't.

But I won't lie... the moment felt good. Not because I hurt him, but because I wasn't powerless anymore.

Weeks have passed. He kept showing up in classes. Then one night, after a tough sparring session, we sat down to cool off and chat. He looked over at me and said, "Where do I know you from?"

I smiled. "Math class," I said.

He blinked, stared, and then it clicked.

Everyone who called me "Lee" knew me from my early years. He didn't know me as Leo.

"Lee…" His voice cracked. "Man, I remember you now. What are you doing with your life these days?"

"I run a water treatment company," I said. "Doing pretty well."

He paused. "When you dropped out, I thought you were just going to crash and burn."

There it was. The honesty. The expectation I'd fail. But I hadn't.

I didn't.

I thrived.

We kept talking. The bitterness I carried began to fade. He admitted he was embarrassed by how he used to treat kids like me. He said that after that first class, he went home asking himself, "What did I do to deserve that?" Now, he said, "I know."

That hit me. Hard.

For so long, I had portrayed him as the villain. But now I saw him differently: a guy shaped by his environment, by the same tough-love system that raised me. He wasn't evil. He was just another man who had once been taught to break others down instead of building them up.

That conversation made me think of something my old friend Jim W. once told me when we were just fifteen:

"We don't have to be just like our fathers."

He said it with so much conviction, and at the time, I didn't fully understand it. But now, it makes perfect sense.

Our fathers, our teachers, wanted us to do well, but they came from a world where emotion was seen as weakness and toughness was survival. They passed down what they knew. But it was up to us to decide what we'd carry forward and what we'd leave behind.

Getting to know that teacher again helped me realize something bigger than karma.

This wasn't about revenge. It was about growth.

It was about healing.

Sometimes, the best kind of justice isn't a punch or payback. It's simply becoming everything they said you never would. And then choosing to rise above it.

That's the thing about struggle: it either hardens you... Or it humbles you.

For me, it did both.

And through it all, every fight, every breakthrough, every rebuilt engine, I learned what school never taught me:

You don't need to be perfect to build something powerful. You just need to keep going.

Forged by Fire

Looking back on everything in this chapter, like cars, school, plumbing, training, and karma, it's clear to me now that I wasn't just learning how to survive. I was learning how to *become.*

Every struggle was like being forged. Every insult, every failure, every punch I threw or took all added up to something, something real and unshakable. I didn't have the diploma, the perfect report card, or the traditional accolades. But I had something else: Fire.

I built my first car before I ever gained confidence in a classroom. I learned how to read people before I could read textbooks. I developed grit under the hood of a Dodge and discipline in a freezing garage with rusted weights and burning lungs. I didn't follow a roadmap; I actually built one.

And along the way, something else happened. I learned how to let go of old pain. Don't forget it, but transform it. I saw the man who once humiliated me ask for help. I looked him in the eye and didn't seek revenge anymore.

Chapter 7:
Dirty Basements and Crawl Spaces

Clean Water Starts in the Dirtiest Spaces

I need to include this part because if you really want to understand what we do, you need to see where this work actually takes place. Installing and servicing water systems isn't glamorous. You won't find it in a glossy brochure or showroom. It's dirty. It's physical. And it takes place in the kinds of environments most people wouldn't crawl into on a dare.

We're talking about pitch-black crawl spaces, basements crawling with spiders, and attics that feel like ovens in the middle of July. We haul heavy tanks down rickety stairs, through moldy basements, and under mobile homes that seem like they're about to collapse on us. Every job was different. Every house has its own personality and its own set of problems. There's no playbook. You adapt. You improvise. You get dirty.

What most folks don't realize is this: **clean water starts in the dirtiest places**. We go where the contamination hides. We dig into the hidden mess so families can have peace of mind at the faucet. This isn't just about installing equipment; it's about restoring safety and health, one nasty crawl space and basement at a time.

If you've never been in this trade, let me show you what it's really about. It's not just about fixing leaks. It's crawling into the guts of buildings, places so filthy and forgotten they seem like scenes from a horror movie. You're working in homes built before the war, squeezing under beams where the air is thick with mildew and regret. Some crawl spaces are so tight,

I've had to dig with a trenching trowel just to make room to breathe.

And it's not just the space, it's what's *living* in it.

I've run into rats, snakes, black widows, brown recluses, fire ants, wasps, you name it. One time, I reached up to my elbow into what looked like insulation and pulled out a dead cat. The maggots from it poured into my sleeve. I gagged so hard I thought I'd lose my lunch. That's an image... you don't forget it. You have nightmares about it for years to come.

Then there's the added issue of fiberglass raining down on you as you crawl through hundred-degree heat. Your skin itches like fire, but you can't stop. The jobs are not done.

Another time, I was crawling alone under an old farmhouse, chasing a broken pipe that ran all the way to the back. I cut the pipe, and suddenly a valve let water spray everywhere. I lunged forward, hand-first, and felt nothing. Just air. I peeled back the insulation and saw it: an old cobblestone well. **Thirty feet deep, which was wide open, with no cover or warning.** If I'd gone a few inches further, I might not be writing this chapter today.

Some places are haunted in more ways than one. I once went back to St. James Catholic School, the same place where, as a kid, I saw something no child should ever have to see or experience: a school shooting. Years later, I was in the basement installing a system. The plaques that once hung in the hallways in the school that honored the victims were now on the floor in the basement. It was cold down there, but not from the weather. It felt eerie, like the past had followed me. I've been bitten, stung, and nearly shot by a homeowner who didn't know I was coming. I've lugged 80-pound salt bags down staircases that threatened to collapse with every step. I've soldered pipe with an open flame, praying the insulation didn't catch fire. Today we've got equipment that is safer to use, like PEX, ProPress, SharkBite, but back then? It was torch, sweat, and hope.

But nothing, and surely nothing, sticks with you like that **first crawl space** job.

My first crawl space job? I'll never forget it. Some guy didn't want to pay for a plumber, so he called me, a young buck only 15, who needed the money, with a wrench and a need to prove myself.

"Just crawl under there and run a new pipe to the kitchen sink," he said. It sounded simple.

Until I saw the jagged hole in the foundation wall, barely wide enough to squeeze through, I dropped to my stomach and crawled in like I was storming Normandy.

The smell hit me first: damp earth, mildew, and something dead. I flicked on my headlamp and was greeted by cobwebs so thick they looked like insulation. My shoulder grazed a pipe wrapped in ancient asbestos. Mice scurried around me. Every inch forward felt like a negotiation with God.

Then something cold touched my leg. I froze.

A Snake.

I almost kicked out the foundation block trying to escape. Turned out it was a black racer, harmless, but it could've been a rattler for all I knew. After I calmed down and figuratively changed my pants, I went back in and finished the job.

I came out hours later, soaked in sweat, covered in dirt, cobwebs, fiberglass, and with a new kind of respect for the underworld we work in.

Because the truth is, crawl spaces are where you find the worst of everything: mold, rot, rodents, and forgotten corners of the American Dream. But they're also where the *real* work gets done. No glory. No air conditioning. Just a flashlight, a tool bag, and a stubborn streak.

This trade? It isn't just plumbing. **It's perseverance.**

When you're down in the dark, crawling through filth, unsure of your footing and completely alone, that's when you find out who you really are.

And let me tell you, **it's not a job for the faint of heart.**

Chapter 8:
Fitting In

Life Lessons in Socialization

I never went to college. Dyslexia made traditional education nearly impossible, but that didn't mean I stopped learning. Life became my classroom, and some of my best lessons came simply by showing up, being around the right people, and learning how to adapt.

Several of my friends went off to college, including the University of Delaware, or "U of D" as we called it. The college town of Newark, Delaware, was just a short drive from where we grew up in New Jersey. On weekends, it became our playground.

Every Friday and Saturday night, Main Street, "The Strip," came alive. We'd cruise up and down in our muscle cars, windows down, music blaring, just looking for the night's fun. At that time, I had a few custom muscle cars that made a statement. They were loud, fast, and drew plenty of attention from both guys and girls.

One of my closest friends during those years was Jamie. We had known each other since we were nine, but we really became close in high school. Jamie actually went to the University of Delaware, and even though I wasn't a student, he always made sure I felt welcome. He'd take me to frat parties and tell people I was from another college in Jersey just to help me blend in. It worked. We dressed sharp, we were big, fit guys, and we looked the part. We never had trouble getting into bars.

We spent many weekends together like that, bouncing between parties, bars, and the State Theater, a $2 movie house that played cult classics like Pink Floyd's The Wall, The Song Remains the Same, and The Rocky Horror Picture Show. My buddy Rob, AKA Muscle-Head, once rode on my car door hanging out the window as we cruised down Main Street trying to impress girls. He even got a ticket for it. We were young, having fun and thought we were invincible.

I may not have been enrolled in college, but I was living the college life. I soaked in every part of it, from the cars to the friendships, to the random stories that only make sense in hindsight.

One of those stories involved Jamie's Porsche 928. It was making a strange noise, so I dropped him off at class and took it to figure out the issue. Under the car, I found a lot of oil and road tar, so I drove it to a self-serve car wash to clean it up. It was cold out, so I threw on one of Jamie's jackets, which had his name on it from karate school. While I was scrubbing the car, a girl nearby saw the name and called me "Jamie." I didn't correct her. We talked for a bit, sat in the car to warm up, and before I left, she asked for my number. I think she liked the car more than me. She spotted Jamie's business card in the center console and took it, thinking it was mine. She left, I got back under the car and found a loose panel, snapped it back in, and the noise was gone. I was a hero for a day.

Later that day, she called and Jamie answered. She started talking like she knew him, and he had no clue who she was. After some confusion, it clicked: I had been the "Jamie" she met. He laughed, but told me if she called back again, he was going to give her my number and address just to mess with me. Luckily for me, she never called again. And I am grateful that caller ID didn't exist yet.

This kind of stuff happened often. But behind the fun and chaos was something real, something meaningful. I was learning how to talk to people from all walks of life. How to blend in. How to fit into worlds that once felt out of reach.

And a huge part of that came from Jamie's family.

A Second Family I'll Never Forget

Jamie wasn't just a friend; he was family. And his family became like a second home to me.

What I remember most about that time wasn't just Jamie; it was his mom, Marie.

Marie was larger than life. If she were still alive today, I'm not sure if she'd get mad at me for saying this or just laugh, but she was the boldest woman I've ever met. If you didn't know her, she could scare the hell out of you. With one look, part Ursula the Sea Witch, part drill sergeant, she could freeze you in your tracks. But if she liked you, you were in. And thank God, she liked me.

One time, when I was about fifteen, my younger brother came with me to Jamie's house. While we were working on something outside, he was inside playing video games. Marie came in, saw him, and in true Marie fashion snapped, "Who the hell are you?" My brother was about to cry. "I'm Lee's brother," he stammered. (Everyone called me Lee back then, since my dad was also Leo.) Marie backed off, but that was her way; intense, protective, with no filter.

Jamie never brought girls home; he knew Marie would run them off before they hit the doorstep.

I walked into their house like I belonged there. Marie would shout from the kitchen, "Go to Wawa and get me a pack of cigarettes and some donuts. Here's the keys, pick whichever car you want." I'd remind her I was fifteen and didn't have a license yet. She'd say, "But you know how to drive. And here's twenty bucks, keep the change." So, I'd take the Cadillac or the Mercedes and do my part.

Jamie's dad, Dr. Atlig, delivered me at birth and was our family doctor. He had a thick Turkish accent, and I remember telling Jamie I couldn't understand half of what he said. Jamie laughed, "Don't worry, I don't either."

They were good people, tight-knit, generous, and well-respected. When I started my own business years later, many of the doctors and lawyers who used to gather for card games at the Atligs' house became my clients. I remember those poker nights in the basement. We'd sit and listen to their stories, and feel like we were part of something bigger.

Jamie also had an older brother, Ramsey, who passed away when he was just seven. He had hydrocephalus, a rare condition involving fluid buildup in the brain. I remember seeing him once at The Mariner (later the Riverview Inn), wearing strange medical gear I'd never seen before. Several kids in our area had similar conditions. I don't think that was a coincidence. Given the toxic water and chemical runoff from the DuPont plant, including benzene, I believe environmental contamination may have played a role. It touched nearly every family we knew.

Over time, Jamie lost his entire immediate family. First Ramsey. Then Marie, when we were in our late twenties. Then, we lost Dr. Atlig when Jamie was in his thirties.

Strangely, both Marie and Dr. Atlig died on the same date, September 2nd, but twelve years apart.

I called Jamie on September 2nd. He tried to sound normal, but I could hear the pain in his voice. He's not one to show emotion, but I've always been more like a brother than just a friend, and he confided in me. That date haunts him.

When I reminded him, I used to be the one bringing Marie her cigarettes and donuts, he cracked a smile and said, "So you're the one!" We both laughed, knowing full well Marie had no shortage of helpers.

When Marie passed, the funeral was packed. But just as they were about to lower her into the ground, the sky erupted. Thunder cracked, lightning lit up the cemetery, and a heavy rainfall made most people rush to their cars. Jamie's family and I stood under the tent, soaked, shivering, and stunned.

"She's not going into the ground quietly," someone said. We believed it.

To this day we joke that Marie must've met Mother Nature in the afterlife and demanded one last show. And boy, did she get it.

Marie, you made your point.

Rest in peace Marie… my second mother.

Looking back now, I realize those years weren't just about fast cars, parties, or pretending I belonged on a college campus. I was learning how to navigate a world that didn't come with a manual, especially for someone like me, a high school dropout with dyslexia and something to prove.

Jamie and his family never judged me for not going the traditional route. Instead, they welcomed me, believed in me, and showed me a version of life I hadn't seen before. From poker nights in a doctor's basement to running errands for the fiercest woman I've ever met, I was soaking up lessons I didn't even know I'd need later.

I wasn't lost. I was learning how to belong, how to carry myself, how to talk to people who lived very different lives from the one I came from.

These moments riding down Main Street, fixing cars, and hearing grown men talk shop over cigars and cards taught me how to adapt, connect, and dream a little bigger than my surroundings.

I may not have earned a degree, but I earned something just as valuable:

The ability to walk into any room, look someone in the eye, and know that I belonged there too.

That's when I stopped surviving and started becoming who I was meant to be.

Chapter 9:
Making Ends Meet

The Hustle of Winter Work

Working with my father was definitely a learning experience, and not all of it was easy. Being a small company, jobs were unpredictable, and we didn't always have steady work, especially during the winter. Construction would slow down, and remodels were few and far between.

I needed something to fill in the gaps.

That's how I ended up working the night shift at a New Jersey Turnpike Service Center near our town. The job involved simple auto service and pumping gas, but the hours were brutal: 11 p.m. to 7 a.m. and in the dead of winter. It was miserable.

I was 18 and about to start my very first night shift. My manager, Gary, handed me the cash drawer (since credit cards weren't used much yet), gave me a brief rundown, and then... vanished. I didn't know where he went, and suddenly I was running the place alone. Cars came in, I pumped gas, handled repairs, and my pockets quickly filled with cash. I gained plenty of service experience, but I'd never run the whole shop.

Around 5 a.m., Gary finally reappeared. Turns out, he went into the back-storage room, locked the door, and passed out. Apparently, that wasn't unusual. I wasn't impressed.

At first, I thought Gary was lazy or unreliable. But I learned the truth quickly: he was working two jobs. His family owned a farm nearby, and during the day, he worked the fields. At night, he was here. He was exhausted. He was just trying to make ends meet. Just like me.

Gary: A Quiet Bond

After a few weeks, Gary and I became friends. He moved to the second shift, and I took over the third. It didn't pay much more, but I earned it simply by showing up. Some nights were dead quiet. I'd call my buddy Rob around 2 a.m. and wake him up just to chat.

"Whatcha doing?" I'd ask.

He'd reply, "I'm at the beach getting a tan, what do you think I'm doing?"

Sometimes he'd hang up on me. We still laugh about those calls today.

Eventually, Gary came by my house. When I introduced him to my mom, she immediately recognized him; his mother had babysat my sister and me when we were little. Gary and I had met as kids. Full Circle.

As the weather warmed up and my dad's business got busier again, I left the night shift behind. But Gary and I stayed close. We worked on cars, went to the track on Sundays, and hung out often. Our girlfriends became friends. Everything felt steady.

Then, Gary's world changed.

The Chain Reaction

One night, Gary broke down. His father had just died of brain cancer. On his deathbed, his father told him something that would haunt Gary:

"It was the pesticides. I'm sure of it."

Back then, we didn't fully understand the dangers of those chemicals. But now, with my knowledge of water filtration and environmental toxins, I know Gary's father was right.

They were spraying poison, not just on the crops, but into the soil, air, and into the water they drank. Gary's father told him to sell the farm and get out. He didn't want his son to suffer the same fate.

Gary listened.

He had just put the farm up for sale. Said he was ready for a new chapter, one with less weight on his shoulders, maybe even a little peace. We talked about it as if it were a fresh start. He seemed lighter, hopeful even. We made plans to work on a friend's car that Sunday, just like old times.

But Sunday came... and Gary didn't.

I waited. I called. No answer. Something felt wrong, but I told myself he probably got busy or sidetracked. He always did things his own way.

Then the phone rang.

It was a buddy of mine, an EMT. His voice was different, flat and hollow. I knew before he said the words.

"There's been an accident," he told me. "It was bad."

And then came the punch that took the breath from my lungs. "It was Gary. He didn't make it."

I nearly dropped the phone. My knees buckled. It was the kind of call that changes you forever. It didn't feel real. It couldn't be.

It happened just down the road from his house. I knew the spot well, an old farm intersection with a single stop sign. It was always flat and wide open, the kind of road where you barely tap the brakes because you could see for a quarter mile in every direction.

But the land had changed.

After Gary gave up farming, the fields were left to grow wild. Weeds six feet high swallowed the view, thick like a wall. He must have pulled out the way he always did: confident, routine, expecting a clear road.

But this time, he couldn't see what was coming.

The other car hit him and was traveling at 50 mph. T-boned. No warning. No chance.

It killed him slowly.

One second, he was here, his life unfolding in a new direction, and the next, he was gone.

Just like that.

He was only 21.

The autopsy was brutal. My friend Jamie's father, who was also the town coroner, told me Gary's ribs had punctured his lungs. He drowned in his own blood. It wrecked me to know what he went through in his final moments, alone in that car.

The Grave and the Lessons

I served as a pallbearer at Gary's funeral. There weren't many of us there, but we carried him together, unlike his father's funeral, where Gary had to carry the coffin almost alone with only two caretakers.

At least this time, his friends were there. I was there.

I remember standing by the grave long after everybody else had walked away. Someone had to come back and grab my hand to get me to move. I just couldn't believe he was gone.

Looking back, I can link every step of the chain that led to Gary's death:

1. His father's illness from the pesticides

2. The decision to stop farming

3. The overgrown fields

4. The blind spot at the intersection

Every cause created an effect. A chain reaction. Just like in The Butterfly Effect, one event leads to another until everything changes.

To this day, I visit Gary's grave. I tell him what's going on in my life. I brought my current wife there when she first visited New Jersey to introduce her, in a way. I've also brought my kids there, too. I showed them the intersection, told them Gary's story, and reminded them that we're not bulletproof. None of us is.

I never imagined losing a friend that young.

I'm grateful for every moment Gary and I had, but I wish we had more.

Rest in peace, Gary. You are missed.

Chapter 10:
Headed South

Chasing opportunity, healing, and a little sunshine.

It was 1989, not long after Gary's death, and my karate buddy Steve had just been honorably discharged from the military. We both needed a change and a reset. So, we planned a trip to Florida to visit a mutual friend who had recently moved there.

What started as a week-long getaway quickly turned into something bigger.

As soon as we arrived, I felt it in my bones that this place was different. The sun, the warmth, the palm trees… it was winter in Jersey, but Florida felt like freedom. A breath of fresh air. I didn't even realize how heavy everything had become until I felt that weight lift in the Florida sun.

We looked at each other and asked the question: "What if we just… stayed."

We checked around for work. I visited a few water treatment companies to see if anyone needed a good installer, and nearly all of them said yes, I could start immediately. Steve found job opportunities, too. That sealed it.

We made the decision. We were moving to Florida.

I was a little nervous about telling my parents I was leaving the family business and heading so far from home, but to my surprise, they were completely supportive. They wanted me to grow. They knew I needed this. That kind of unconditional support stays with you forever.

So, we packed up our things, Steve in his car, me in my van, and hit the road south. We weren't just driving to Florida. We were driving toward something new.

Starting Over in Wellington

We rented a townhouse in Wellington, just outside West Palm Beach. The place wasn't much to look at, no furniture, no couch, just some beds and a makeshift TV stand built from cinder blocks and wooden boards we found in the shed.

But we didn't care. We were here. We were free. We were starting something.

I narrowed my job search down to two water treatment companies, but couldn't decide which one to choose. I asked if I could subcontract for them using my own tools and van. I didn't want to sign a non-compete contract; I was already thinking long-term, about owning my own business one day.

Both companies said yes.

Every morning, I'd stop in to pick up equipment, load my van, and head out to install water systems all over South Florida. It was good work, and I was good at it. But Florida's heat was no joke. One day, I was working on a remote property with no water, no electricity installed yet, and no stores nearby. I was sweating through my shirt, dizzy, and close to heat stroke. When I finally arrived at a convenience store, I downed two bottles of water before I even reached the counter to pay.

From that day on, I never went to a job without packing more water than I thought I'd need.

The thought that stuck in my head was:

"How would it sound if H2O Leo died of dehydration?"

Doormen by Night, Entrepreneurs by Day

One afternoon, Steve and I were sparring in the courtyard outside our townhouse when our neighbor Paul walked by. He saw us throwing punches and kicks and asked what the hell we were doing. Once he realized we were trained fighters, not maniacs, he asked if we wanted to work at the nightclub, which he managed in West Palm Beach.

We agreed to the offer. The place was called Cruzan Liquor Stand, and Paul needed doormen who could keep the peace.

The job paid cash. We got to eat for free. And we weren't out spending money every weekend. It was a win-win situation.

But it wasn't always calm. We had many wild encounters. One night, a rowdy baseball team in town for spring training started a brawl, and Steve and I had to toss a few of them out. We earned our money that night and plenty of bruises, too.

But honestly, we were living the dream.

By day, we were working with water systems. By night, we were keeping the peace at the club and met people from all over the country. The nightlife, the beaches, the women… it was like a different universe compared to our small hometown.

We had found paradise.

The Goodbye

But like most good things, it didn't last forever.

Steve decided he wanted to go back up north as he did not adjust as well as I did. Suddenly, I was on my own, no roommate, no one to split the bills. Then, my girlfriend and I broke up. I would say she made me a better man.

But I was 21. She was 30. The timing was not right for us both. She was "The one that got away."

Heartbroken and alone, I got a visit from my dad.

Years before, he had worked in the same area of Florida. He came to check on me. And after spending a few days together, he sat me down and said:

"I'm not getting any younger, and I could use your help back home."

He didn't guilt-trip me. He just told me the truth. And deep down, I knew it was time. I needed to come back to my roots.

So, when the lease ended, I packed up my van and headed north again, back to New Jersey. Back to the family. Back to the business.

The first winter back was brutal. Freezing. Gray. Bleak.

And all I could think about were palm trees, ocean air, and warm sand.

When the Road Calls You Home

Looking back on this chapter of my life, it's clear that some of the biggest growth doesn't happen in comfort; it happens in transition. I didn't know it at the time, but losing Gary, moving to Florida, falling in love, and returning home… it was all part of a bigger process. A forging.

I learned that change doesn't wait until you're ready; it shows up when it's needed.

Gary's death cracked something open in me. It reminded me that life is short and that we don't always get second chances. Florida was my escape, but also my testing ground. I proved to myself that I could build a life anywhere. That I could adapt, hustle, take risks, and still stand tall when things fell apart.

I learned how to build a business before I even realized I was becoming a businessman.

I learned how to let go of comfort, of people, of plans.

And most importantly, I learned that going back home doesn't mean failure. Sometimes, it's the most courageous thing you can do.

Florida showed me freedom.

But New Jersey reminded me of who I was and who I still had yet to become.

Chapter 11:
Love, Legacy and the Life We Built

The day I stopped building muscle cars and started building a family.

Coming back from Florida wasn't part of the plan, but life has a funny way of putting you right where you're meant to be. I had returned home feeling heavy-hearted, unsure of my next move. That's when my sister Cindy called me with a wild idea: a blind date.

"Her name's M," she said. "She's the sister of my friend from work."

I wasn't exactly in the mood for romance. I was still readjusting to life back in New Jersey, missing the Florida sun and nursing the wounds of a recent breakup. But I figured, what did I have to lose?

The plan was to go with my sister and brother-in-law to meet this mystery girl on a Sunday afternoon. As we drove, I started to get that nervous energy. What if I didn't like her? What if it was awkward? What if I were stuck there all day trying to make small talk?

I shared my concerns, and we made a pit stop at the liquor store to calm my nerves. My brother-in-law grabbed a 12-pack of Heineken and made me a deal: "If the date doesn't work out, you don't owe me a thing. But if it does, you owe me a new 12-pack."

Fair enough. We shook on it.

When we arrived, M wasn't downstairs yet. I sat in the living room, making small talk, nursing a beer, and wondering what I'd gotten myself into. Then I saw her coming down the stairs, and just like that, the nerves melted away.

She was stunning. Petite, with blond hair and a spark in her eyes. Funny enough, we were both wearing matching colors; my shirt matched her pants, and my pants matched her top. Some people call it a coincidence. I call it fate.

We sat there talking under the awkward stares of our sisters, so we decided to take a walk around the neighborhood. It was a chilly early spring in Jersey, which is nothing like Florida weather, and eventually we ducked into her car to warm up and talk more.

By the time we got back, my sister had already left. I was stranded, but M didn't mind. She offered to drive me home, and honestly, I didn't want the night to end either.

That night started a whirlwind romance.

We lived about 120 miles apart, with me in South Jersey and her in North Jersey, but that didn't slow us down at all. We made it work. Weekend visits turned into weekday phone calls. Long drives became routine. And when we were together, it just felt right.

By the end of the year, just eight months after that blind date, we got married. M always dreamed of a Christmas wedding, so we made it happen. December 1991. It was small, intimate, and full of meaning. We didn't need anything extravagant, only the people who mattered and a little bit of laughter. And we got both. M wanted to get married with her hair in its natural color, so she dyed it for the wedding. Some of my friends called her Fran, like the TV show The Nanny, if you remember that show, it's funny. She sounded just like her, just try to get that sound out of your head.

We tied the knot at a courthouse in Maryland. M, nervous but glowing, made us all laugh when she accidentally called me her "awful, wedded husband" instead of "lawful." It's one of those moments that stick, and it became a running joke in our family for years, and every time we watched the wedding video, we laughed like it had just happened.

My dad stood beside me as my best man. My sister Cindy and her husband were there, along with my brother Steven. M's sister, Lisa and my oldest friend, Chris, who also happened to be our wedding photographer, were there too. Chris and I had known each other since we were five. His dad worked with mine, and we grew up together. That made it even more special.

M and I were young, in love, and ready to take on the world.

We jumped into married life like we did everything else, fast and full of heart. M didn't just become my wife; she became my partner in every sense. She helped me run the water treatment business, handling phone calls, scheduling jobs, and managing customers like a pro. She had a sharp mind, and she wasn't afraid to get her hands dirty.

We were a team.

And before long, it was time to grow our team.

At the age of 25, I became a father. Leo Jr was born, and nothing could have prepared me for the flood of emotions that came with that moment. Holding him in my arms, I felt something shift deep inside me, a sense of responsibility, pride, and fierce love that rewired everything I thought I knew about life.

However, almost immediately, we were hit with our first challenge. Within days of bringing him home, Leo turned yellow, and he developed Jaundice. His bilirubin levels were dangerously high, close to 50. The doctors told us he might need a blood transfusion, and because it was the early 1990s, that meant potential exposure to HIV or other infections. They even handed me a waiver to sign, acknowledging those risks.

I froze.

This was my son. My firstborn. No way was I going to let that happen without exhausting every other option.

I contacted doctors I trusted, people who had helped my family in the past. They recommended trying phototherapy first: ultraviolet light to break down the bilirubin. If it didn't work, then we'd consider the transfusion.

After just a few hours of the light treatment, his numbers dropped significantly. After 48 hours, he was back in the safe zone with no transfusion needed. That moment changed me forever. It was the first time I learned to question the system, to stand up, ask better questions, and fight for the people I love. Especially my kids.

That's when I began buckling down, not just as a worker or a husband, but as a father.

Three years later, Dean joined the family. With Dean, we didn't take any chances. We used phototherapy as a precaution, and thankfully, he was healthy from the start.

Dean was a tough little guy who was strong-willed and curious. He was always by my side, mimicking me with his  toy tools while I worked on cars or something around the house. He wasn't the hugging type, instead, he'd show affection by head-butting you, like a little football player. That was just his way, and we loved it.

Then, just when we thought life couldn't get any fuller, along came our daughter, Nadine.

She was beautiful from the moment she arrived, and she changed the rhythm of our home completely. A family friend gifted her a wind-up mobile that played "You Are My Sunshine." I must've wound that thing up a thousand times. I hummed it so often; it became the background music of my life.

One day, I was working with my dad on a job installing a water system in a basement, and I caught myself humming the tune. He stopped, smiled, and said, "You know, that was your grandfather's favorite song. He used to sing it to all the grandkids." And I could tell my dad liked it too. We all did. Like father like son.

I paused for a second and felt something deep within my chest.

My daughter's lullaby... was also my grandfather's. Like life had once again come full circle.

From Tradesman to Protector

How fatherhood gave my work new meaning.

By the time Nadine was born, I was thirty years old and locked in not just as a father and husband, but as a man with a mission. My growing family gave me something bigger to fight for.

Our family water treatment company was thriving. We were busy working in both Delaware and New Jersey, tackling toxic wells, buried chemical drums, and leaking fuel tanks from gas stations. The mess left behind by decades of careless industry was everywhere. The need for clean water to purify all these toxins was huge.

I'd seen the impact of contamination firsthand. People were getting sick, and kids were fighting diseases they should've never been exposed to. Entire neighborhoods were poisoned without even knowing it. And the worst part, the government didn't have the resources or sometimes the will to do much about it.

So, I made it personal.

We began developing filtration systems that could neutralize the effects of acid rain, balance pH levels, reduce VOCs, and remove heavy metals and other toxins. We didn't just sell systems, we solved problems. I worked tirelessly to make sure every family we helped would never have to worry about what was coming out of their tap.

One job I'll never forget was in Greenville, Delaware, one of the wealthiest neighborhoods in the state. I was asked to keep the test results confidential. The client didn't want the lab to know whose water it was. The results came back with 26 different VOCs (volatile organic compounds), with some over 100 times the legal limit.

Turns out, the property was owned by the very same company that manufactured the chemicals polluting the area.

Talk about irony.

They were drinking their own poison.

There was a saying in my old neighborhood, which had earned the unfortunate title of a "cancer cluster." When people got sick, they would say, "There must be something in the water."

And I'd always say, "Not my water, I have a filter."

It started as a joke. Now it was a mission.

Toxic Awakening: The danger I faced. The decision I made.

It was the early 1990s when I started doing more and more work inside the chemical plants scattered across South Jersey and Delaware. These places resembled small cities, industrial giants tucked behind fences and guarded gates. And while the pay was decent, the risks were enormous.

We were working on a project at DuPont Chambers Works in Deepwater, NJ, called "Sewer in the Sky." The goal was to reroute the runoff water that would normally flow into open ditches and eventually into the Delaware River. On paper, it sounded like a noble project. In reality, I was stepping into one of the most toxic environments on the East Coast.

The Delaware River had already been labeled the 9th most toxic river in the world. Not just in the U.S., but in the world. Think about that. And here I was, crawling through pipes, welding joints, and breathing in fumes that would make your eyes water and your throat burn.

The first real scare happened right after lunch one day.

I was walking back to my job site and unknowingly walked straight into a cloud of phosgene gas, also known as mustard gas. The moment I inhaled, I got sick instantly, vomiting, disoriented, and dizzy. I scrambled to find a windsock and get upwind.

A chemical plant worker rushed over to me and asked, "Do you smoke?"

"No," I replied, confused.

"Good," he said. "You'll heal faster."

I could smell my own burned lung flesh coming out of my mouth. They sent me to the infirmary, checked me out, and gave me a couple of days off with pay. That was it. No real treatment, no outside report, no hospital visit. If you could walk out under your own power, it wasn't considered an incident.

That was just one of many incidences.

At DuPont's Edgemoor Plant in Delaware, I witnessed a chlorine gas explosion that could have killed dozens. We were working five stories up. One of the tanks blew out, and gas was everywhere. My crew and I had to slide down the exterior rails like something out of an action movie just to get out alive. If we hadn't been young and fast, we wouldn't have made it.

Another time, we were working in a cyanide plant. I was down in a sump, basically a giant pit used to house pumps, with a coworker. Without warning, cyanide gas started leaking in. My lips turned blue. My African American coworker turned pale. We were suffocating. We sounded the alarm and got hoisted out just in time. Another trip to the infirmary. Another "couple of days off with pay."

Back then, we thought we were lucky.

Now I know we were just walking dead men who happened to dodge the bullet that day.

The Final Straw

It was a freezing morning in 1995, with temperatures possibly as low as five degrees, and I was 70 feet in the air on a steel beam, doing steam trace work to keep the pipes from freezing. I had a Lineman's toolbox on my shoulder that weighed about 50 pounds.

And I wasn't tethered. I slipped.

The toolbox fell and exploded on the ground. Thank God it didn't hit anyone. As for me, I somehow managed to wrap my arms and legs around the beam like a spider and hold on. Though it was only for a few minutes, it felt like an hour that I clung there. Not just to the steel but to life itself.

In those minutes, everything flashed through my mind:

1. The mustard gas.
2. The chlorine explosion.
3. The cyanide pit.
4. The asbestos pipes.
5. My kids.
6. My wife.

What was I doing?

Why was I still here, risking everything?

Eventually, one of my coworkers clipped me in with a tether and helped me back to safety. But the kicker was that I had to go report the incident to the Head of Safety.

And that's when I walked into the office and saw my MOM sitting behind the desk. She had taken a job at the same plant. The look on her face said everything: relief, rage, heartbreak.

That day, I looked her in the eye and said, "I'm done. I'm never working in another chemical plant again."

And I meant it.

From that moment forward, I focused all my energy on clean water. I poured every ounce of grit, ingenuity, and heart into building a business that would protect and not poison people. My mission became clear:

No family should have to drink toxic water. Not on my watch.

The days of risking my life in chemical plants were behind me. I had already seen too much mustard gas, chlorine gas, and cyanide exposure. I was done gambling with my health and my future.

Building the Dream: The Birth of the Water Business

No more near-death jobs. It was time to build something that could truly change lives.

After that final chemical plant incident, I was done risking everything for a paycheck. I had three beautiful children. I had a growing sense of purpose. And I had something else, a vision.

I knew water. Not just the pipes and fittings, but also their chemistry, their dangers, and, more importantly, how to fix them. I had been in the trenches, quite literally. I'd seen firsthand how contamination destroyed communities, made people sick, and took lives. And I had seen what worked to stop it.

Now, I was going to turn all that hard-won knowledge into something powerful. Something lasting.

It didn't happen overnight. At first, I started small. I took subcontracting jobs and ran installations under other companies while slowly building up my own client base. I learned everything I could about running a business, like how to price jobs, manage inventory, and make customers feel like family. I didn't have a business degree, but I had grit, instinct, and hustle, and that was more than enough.

And the word spread fast.

Because when you fix someone's water, when you truly give them peace of mind, they remember you. They tell their neighbors. Their family. Their friends. Before long, I was working not just in homes but in schools, office buildings, farms, and massive estates. Some clients were wealthy. Others were barely getting by. But I treated them all the same because everyone deserves clean water.

It Was Never Just About Business

Every install, every test, every filter I placed into someone's home felt like I was undoing a bit of damage from the past. I wasn't just installing equipment. I was installing safety, Health, and Hope.

And it started to grow. The company evolved from a one-man show with a van full of tools into something far bigger.

I hired a team. Trained them myself. Taught them the science, the craftsmanship, and the heart behind what we do.

Because to me, this wasn't just plumbing. It wasn't just filtration.

It was a calling.

And when I saw my sons playing in the yard, laughing under the sprinkler, drinking from the tap without fear, I knew why I did it. I knew that every toxic job, every bad boss, every near-death moment had led me here. It had carved the path.

I wasn't just fixing water. I was protecting futures.

Starting with my own family and extending to thousands of others.

Then I had this reflection, that *My True Path Wasn't written in Blueprints, It Was Written in Water.*

Looking back now, it's clear that the greatest turning point in my life didn't come from a classroom or a promotion; it came from nearly falling off a steel beam, a toolbox crashing to the ground below, and my life hanging by a thread.

That moment forced me to see everything clearly.

I realized I had been trading my life for a paycheck. I was surviving, not thriving. And I wasn't just risking my own life anymore; I had three little ones watching me. Learning from me. Needing me.

It wasn't enough to provide. I had to protect.

And clean water became the means by which I did that.

I didn't come from privilege. I didn't have Ivy League mentors or business school handbooks. But I had a purpose. I had work ethics. And I had a reason to get up every day and give my 110%. That reason had many names, including Leo Jr., Dean, and Nadine. And a family legacy that I was rewriting, one installment at a time.

Some people inherit a family crest.

I inherited a wrench, a mission, and the will to fight for better.

I used to think strength meant being tough enough to survive anything.

Now I know it means being brave enough to change everything.

This wasn't just about building a business.

It was about building something that would outlive me.

Chapter 12:
Itchy Foot and The River Dream

The Beacon of Light in the Widow's Watch

In the late 1990s, I was transitioning from following strictly in my father's footsteps as a plumber and diving headfirst into my own water filtration business. Plumbing jobs were still great locally, but the real growing demand was in the outlying areas. Homes with well water were everywhere, and no one was treating city water at that time because people assumed it was already treated and safe.

In these rural communities, families were dealing with low pH levels, high iron, and manganese in their water. It showed up in their sinks and tubs, causing staining, bad odors, and ruined plumbing. My company at that time, Aqua 1: Your #1 Water Quality Choice, was taking off, and I was finally starting to experience some real success. That success allowed me to enjoy something I haven't had in a while: free time.

Weekends became a sacred thing, and my friends and I would gather on the banks of the Delaware River at my friend Jim McMahon's place. Jim had a little house project right on the Jersey side of the river. He didn't live in it, but he was always working on it. It was always in some state of construction, with tools everywhere, sawdust on the floors, and extension cords snaking through every room. That sawdust had a funny way of sticking to our bare feet, so we jokingly called it The Itchy Foot. The name stuck. "Meet you at The Itchy Foot" became our rallying cry for good times.

We'd spend weekends there boating, riding jet skis, cooking out, and just letting the stress melt away. That little house became the heartbeat of our weekends. One day Jim came to me and said he had to sell it as his life had taken a turn, and he needed to move on. I didn't even hesitate to agree to buy it, because I wanted it.

I had no idea how I'd buy it, but I knew I would.

Jim introduced me to his old friend, who also happened to be his banker. I went to meet him at the local bank and expected the usual stacks of paperwork, background checks, and credit report deep dives. But instead, the banker sat me down with a pen and pad, did the application verbally, and asked me a handful of questions. One question stood out: "Are you going to have Jim help you finish this project?" I paused carefully and said, "No." I didn't want to offend Jim, but I had to be honest. I told the banker that Jim could do the floors as he was great at that, but I'd handle the rest.

The banker looked up, smiled, and flipped the pad around. All he had written was a big smiley face. "You're approved," he said, just like that. That handshake deal taught me one of the best lessons in life: knowing the right people and always telling the truth, even when it's uncomfortable, makes the biggest difference.

It turned out the house was in worse shape than I expected. I had planned to finish what Jim had started, but after a week on-site, I realized the entire place had to be demolished. Back to the bank I went. I asked the same banker for more funding to tear down and build a new house. He thought about it for a second, laughed, and said, "If I were you, I'd do the same thing." More funds approved. Another handshake and I was off and running.

The property was right on the water, and during high tide, the waves from passing cargo ships would flood our job site. We didn't fully understand the toxicity of the river back then, but we knew better than to swim in it. We kept our fun to boating and long evenings on the deck.

My childhood neighbor, Jimmy Luciano, who, yes, was related to Lucky, joined me as a subcontractor. My dad had suggested I call him, and I was grateful when he said yes. Jimmy had babysat me when I was a kid and still called me Elroy from the Jetsons cartoon.

Construction started in the fall of 1997. It took two full years to complete, and it was a massive project. We battled the tide, the weather, and even a few lawsuits from neighbors who didn't like how big the house was becoming. It ended up being three stories tall with a rooftop widow's watch. I might've fudged the height a bit; the town limit was 35 feet, but let's just say we got close. Real close.

In February of 1997, Jimmy and I went to the Philly Boat Show and walked away with a Scarab "go-fast" boat. That thing could hit 80 mph on the river, and we used it as an excuse to take too many days off. If the sun was shining,

Jimmy would show up and say, "Elroy, cancel the day we're going boating." We knew the river so well that we could navigate it in our sleep. But one night, while heading home at high speed, we nearly hit a buoy because its light was out. It scared the hell out of us and reminded me just how fast fun can turn dangerous. Still, the memories were golden.

We had made so many great memories together and created a friendship that would last a lifetime that when Jimmy was ready to sell his boat, naturally I purchased it.

As the house was taking shape, I hired one of my best friends to help, Chris, my friend since we were five. My uncle lent me heavy equipment for demolition and site prep. My dad helped run the machines. We tore down the old house and saved what we could, especially the expensive windows, and filled up four massive dumpsters with debris.

What started as a modest project turned into a dream house. I'd visit high-end homes through my water treatment business, taking mental snapshots of the best features. I laid it all out on a simple CAD program and designed a space that reflected who I was, how far I had come, and where I wanted my family to grow.

I installed a skylight in the rooftop window's watch and kept a light on every night. When we'd return home by boat in the dark, I could spot that light from miles away. It always guided us safely home.

At that time in my life, everything felt aligned. I had a beautiful home, a thriving business, and a family I loved more than life itself. For a whole year, we were living the dream.

But life, as always, was about to test me again, this time in ways I never could've imagined.

A House on the River, A Lesson in Life

Building the Itchy Foot House wasn't just about bricks, beams, and permits; it was about learning what it meant to create something lasting. It was my first new home, built not only with blood, sweat, and tears, but with love, hope, and dreams for the future. Every piece of that house held a story, whether it was the days we skipped work to go boating, or the mornings we scrambled to beat the tide so we could pour a foundation.

It was a time of growth, of stepping into new roles as a father, a husband, and a leader in my own business. I was learning what it meant to balance ambition with responsibility, dreams with reality. And looking back now, I can see that building that home wasn't just about creating a space for my family; it was about proving to myself that I could rise above the odds. I could create beauty and stability in a world that once felt uncertain and unfair.

The river gave me peace, but it also reminded me of the undercurrents always moving beneath the surface of life. Calm one day, stormy the next. You don't control the water; you learn to respect it just as you learn to respect your own journey.

I didn't know what challenges were coming next, but at that moment, with the music playing and the river shimmering in the distance, I was proud. I had taken a worn-down shell of a house and turned it into a sanctuary. A place for my children to grow up, for friends to gather, and for dreams to take shape.

And that beacon of light in the widow's watch

That wasn't just to guide our boat home.

It was to remind me always that no matter how rough the waters got, I knew where home was.

Chapter 13:
Love, Lies and Legal Ties

A Challenging Situation and a New Start

A wise friend once said that if your marriage can survive building a house, it can withstand anything. I believed that. As our dream home rose along the serene banks of the Delaware River, I envisioned a life filled with graduations, weddings, and peaceful family moments. I thought our future was a story of hard work paying off.

But life, it turned out, had its own script.

The Unraveling

The pressures of building a business, raising three children, and managing every aspect of our lives slowly eroded our marriage. I was busy providing and protecting, but while I was fighting for our future, my wife, was slipping away. These changes in our marriage came not with a loud crash but insidiously in the form of phone records.

Despite being cautious of threats from outside, I overlooked what was happening within our close circle. JB, a respected District Attorney and friend, had quietly grown closer to M, disguising his intentions beneath compliments and camaraderie.

The first red flag came from M's brother-in-law, Chris. He noticed strange, late-night calls on his family's phone bill. M had been borrowing a family member's phone so the calls wouldn't appear on our bill. It was Chris' phone plan, and he grew suspicious of the pattern.

I knew someone who might have been able to help an old friend who had previously served as District Attorney.

Coincidentally, he was now married to JB's ex-wife. I asked him to meet with me, and he agreed. I showed him the numbers, but he wasn't sure if they were JB's.

Then, without hesitation, he picked up the phone and called his wife, JB's ex-wife. Reluctantly, she read off all the phone numbers she knew: JB's home line, car phone, work number, pager, and his cell. Every single one matched up with the calls on the log Chris had given me.

That's when it all clicked, and my world fell apart.

Confrontation and Collapse

The revelation hit me like a freight train. Everything we had built, our home, our family, our business, was falling apart. I felt as though I was drowning in betrayal, rage, and an overwhelming sense of loss.

Desperate for clarity, I turned to my lifelong friend and lawyer. He saw my anguish, and rather than lecture me, he quietly reached for a book sitting on the corner of his desk. It was The Art of War by Sun Tzu. He opened it, read aloud, and looked me square in the eyes:

"Stand by the river and wait for the bodies of your enemies to float by."

He didn't need to explain; it said everything. The meaning was crystal clear: stay calm, stay sharp, and let justice reveal itself in time. It was the most unexpected legal advice I'd ever received, and the most powerful.

I acted swiftly. I dismissed M from our company, changed the locks, and began preparing for the storm. JB retaliated, using his position to have me evicted from my home and separated from my children under false accusations.

I needed space to think. I went to my parent's home in Florida seeking solace, safety, and distance from the chaos.

I also hired a private investigator to gather undeniable proof of the affair. In the warmth of Florida, I found clarity. Being in the warm embrace of my parents became my anchor.

The Reckoning

When I returned to New Jersey, my lawyer and I were ready. During a tense settlement meeting with M and JB, my lawyer calmly laid out everything, every photo, timestamp, and call log. JB tried to play it cool, denying everything with rehearsed confidence. But when my lawyer pulled out the photos and call logs, all perfectly matched up, JB's face changed. His mask slipped. His hands shook. His words faltered.

As JB's lawyer yelled at him outside the meeting room, I overheard them. My lawyer leaned over to me and whispered with a satisfied smile, "Never lie to your lawyer."

I allowed myself a brief smile, a moment of justice amid the pain.

Remarkably, the divorce was finalized in just three weeks, an unheard-of timeframe for such a complex situation. Even M's lawyer eventually withdrew, unwilling to risk his own career by defending her. When he tried to bill me later, I refused. I paid enough.

Karma, it seemed, had a sense of humor. One night at a local restaurant, The Riverview Inn, I spotted M's former lawyer who after arguing with his wife walked out and left her there alone. So, I sent her a drink, not out of cruelty, but with a quiet sense of irony. She waved as a way of saying thank you. I could not help myself. I walked over and asked her to dance. She gave me her hand, and off we went. There was a great slow song playing. It was short, symbolic, and very public. My version of a victory lap.

But even with a legal win, emotionally, I was gutted. The kids were torn between two worlds, and I missed them more than words could say.

That 12-pack of Heineken my brother-in-law bought me for the blind date all those years ago. I paid him back, just like we agreed, if the relationship worked out. But after all this, I don't think I'll ever drink Heineken again. LOL.

As each "body" floated past, just as Sun Tzu described, I realized something important. The river, our river, was still flowing. And so was I.

This wasn't the end.

It was the beginning of something new.

Serendipity in the South

After the dust of divorce had settled, after the betrayal, the legal war, the unraveling of everything I thought was solid, I needed to breathe again. I needed sunshine, warmth, and familiarity. I needed Florida.

98

Florida had always been a place of healing for me. After Gary's death, those sun-soaked roads and family hugs helped put the broken pieces of my heart back together. So now, at another breaking point in my life, it has called me again.

I asked my former wife if I could take Leo Jr. with me to visit Mom-Mom and Pop-Pop. She agreed with the condition that he be back before school restarted. I promised we would. So, we packed up, and with a heavy heart and a hopeful spirit, we hit the road.

I drove straight through seventeen hours, through the night. It wasn't just a road trip; it was a pilgrimage back to something familiar and safe. Leo Jr. slept soundly beside me while I powered through, only stopping for fuel and food. As we approached our destination, a long freight train stopped us just before my parents' neighborhood. That's when Leo Jr. stirred, cranky and groggy from the ride. "I wanna go home," he mumbled through his tears.

"We're almost there, buddy," I said. "We're going to see Mom-Mom."

His eyes lit up. In that moment, I realized we both needed this trip more than we knew.

I collapsed onto my parents' couch the second we arrived. Moments later, my brother, whom I hadn't seen in years, kicked my foot and said, "C'mon, we're going for a beer." I wanted to sleep, but something told me to go. We ended up at a local spot where his wife worked. The bright Florida sun outside had left me temporarily blind, walking into the dark bar, and as I went to sit, I missed my stool entirely, landing flat on my back.

And that's when I saw her.

Laughing, radiant, and reaching out her hand to help me up was LeAnn. Blonde hair, blue eyes, and this incredible

99

presence that stole the air from my lungs. "I just met you, and you're already falling for me," she teased with a smile that could melt iron.

In that ridiculous, unforgettable moment, something shifted.

Over the next few days, we were inseparable. She was dealing with her own ghosts, an abusive relationship she was just stepping away from. And I was still picking up the pieces of my shattered life. We weren't looking for love, but we found connection, laughter, and something that felt like a beginning.

Florida wrapped me in warmth again. Between time with my parents, reconnecting with my brother, and the unexpected joy of LeAnn's company, I started to feel like myself again. Like maybe the worst was behind me.

When it came time to leave, I asked LeAnn to visit me in New Jersey. She wasn't sure, as she was still healing, but she said she'd think about it. I hugged my parents, loaded up Leo Jr., and headed back north with more hope than I'd felt in months.

Back home, I remained civil with my ex-wife for the kids' sake. I asked her, "If I moved to Florida, would you let the kids come live with me once I'm settled?" She hesitated but said she'd consider it.

That was enough for me to start planning.

That trip reminded me of the power of new beginnings. What started as an escape from pain became a journey of rediscovery. Florida didn't just offer warmth and beaches; it offered clarity… and LeAnn. She was proof that even in the most unexpected places, there's still magic waiting to be found.

Chapter:14:
The Voice That Changed Everything

Sometimes, all it takes is one voice to remind you who you really are.

At that time in my life, I wasn't just looking for someone to talk to, as I was searching for a soul who could truly see me. Not just hear the words I said, but feel the weight behind them. I didn't need advice or judgment. I needed warmth. I needed understanding. I needed someone I could open up to fully, someone who would hold my heart gently and not let it break further.

That someone was LeAnn.

Our connection started over long-distance phone calls that stretched late into the night. Those conversations became my lifeline. We didn't just talk, we shared. We unraveled old wounds, explored new hopes, and imagined what life could be if we dared to dream again. There was something sacred about it, like we were rebuilding each other one word at a time. It wasn't just emotional, it was soul-deep.

LeAnn was going through her own storm, and during one of our calls, I invited her to come up to New Jersey for a break to breathe, to heal, just to be. My house was quiet then, empty of the usual laughter of kids, but it rested peacefully on the water, surrounded by stillness and space for reflection. I offered it as a safe place for her to gather herself.

She came as a friend... but life, in its beautiful mystery, had more in store. We fell in love not fast, but fully. With honesty. With gratitude. With a quiet knowing that we had found something rare and real.

Spunky and LeAnn

Letting Go to Start Fresh

Love has a way of asking us to take leaps of faith. Not blindly but bravely. And loving LeAnn gave me the strength to make one of the hardest decisions of my life.

I sold the company I had built from the ground up across four states: New Jersey, Delaware, Pennsylvania, and Maryland. It was my life's work, a reflection of years of hustle, sweat, and sacrifice. Letting it go was like watching a part of myself walk away. The sale wasn't ideal; I barely got thirty cents on the dollar, but I found comfort in knowing my clients would be in good hands.

Then came the even deeper cut: I put my dream home on the market. That house wasn't just wood and windows. It held my memories, my plans, my visions of birthdays, holidays, and family milestones. It was supposed to be the "forever place." But the truth was, forever had changed. And as painful as it was to let it go, I knew the most important foundation I could build now was with LeAnn, wherever that would be.

So together, we turned the page. And headed south.

Port St. Lucie and The Promise of a New Life

A year into our journey, we found a place to plant new roots, our first home together in Port St. Lucie, Florida. It wasn't grand, but it was ours. The sunlight felt warmer there, the days felt lighter, and for the first time in what felt like forever, the future didn't look so heavy.

Starting over wasn't easy. I was still healing from the wreckage of divorce, still working through the ache of everything I had let go. But through it all, LeAnn stood by me, and that made the weight easier to carry.

Despite everything, my former wife and I made a choice to remain friends not just for convenience, but for our kids. Because they mattered more than pride or pain, so, as often as I could, I made that 18-hour drive back to New Jersey just to be with them for a few precious days. And every single time I said goodbye, it tore me up inside.

But I knew why I was doing it. I was building something solid, something stable, something worth the distance. I wasn't just starting a new chapter; I was building a new legacy. One rooted in love, sacrifice, and hope.

And it all began with a voice on the other end of the line... the voice I needed.

Back to Water and Roadblocks

I knew I needed to rebuild fast. Water work was my bread and butter. But every company I interviewed in Florida required a five-year non-compete clause. That was a nonstarter. I wasn't about to chain myself to a desk when I knew I had something greater to build.

One day, LeAnn and I went to the Palm Beach Yacht Show. She knew how much I missed being on the water. Among the towering yachts  and gleaming ships, I stumbled across a booth for a marine company, installing AC systems and water makers, essentially large-scale reverse osmosis systems for yachts.

When the manager asked if I needed a water-maker, I laughed. I did not have a boat. Definitely not one that would need a water maker. But we got to talking, and when I mentioned my background in medical-grade water systems for dialysis, he lit up. "You want a job?" he asked. Just like that, I was back in the water game on yachts, this time. I signed a marine-only non-compete, which was perfect, because my focus was still on homes and commercial buildings.

The Nightclub Hustle

To speed things up financially, I picked up a second job, Security at a nightclub in Stuart, Florida. At 6'4" and 235 pounds with years of martial arts, strength training, and some years ago bouncing under my belt, I fit the role well. The owner, Susan, personally interviewed me. I was honest about my experience, and she hired me on the spot.

Within months, I outlasted the revolving door of bouncers and was called into Susan's office. I thought I was getting canned, but instead, she offered me the head of security position, my first big break in Florida.

MMA, Mayhem, and Real-World Self-Defense

Martial arts weren't just something I picked up to pass the time. For me, they were a foundation discipline, structure, and a way to turn fear into control. They shaped who I was from the inside out.

I spent years training in different disciplines. Karate and Aikido gave me focus. Jiu-jitsu taught me technique. Weightlifting gave me strength. And life gave me plenty of opportunities to put it all to the test. Some of that testing even happened right in the dojo. A few local law enforcement officers would join us to practice worst-case scenarios and control techniques. One time, I played the role of a suspect. The officer tried to cuff me, but left an opening. Instinct kicked in, I reversed the hold, locked him up, and snapped the cuffs on him instead. The whole class erupted. It was funny, but it was also a lesson. One missed detail can flip the script instantly.

That lesson became even more valuable when I took that second job working in nightclub security in Stuart, Florida. Chaos doesn't give you time to plan. It shows up uninvited, and it's up to you to either stay calm or get crushed.

When I was promoted to head of security, I knew I needed a team I could trust. So, I turned to the gym. I had been training with some serious guys, UFC fighters, disciplined, humble, and tough as nails. I asked if any of them wanted to work security with me. To my surprise, they all did. Even my instructor. I hired one that day, and two more within weeks. We weren't just a team, we were a unit.

Susan, the owner of the club, was a little nervous. She wasn't sure about having trained fighters in her place, but I assured her: these were good men. They weren't looking for trouble. They just wanted purpose and respect.

Our approach was calculated. My tactic for removing a disruptive guest was simple: I'd lean in and say, "I can't hear you with the music, come up front so we can talk." That walk to the front door gave us space, and gave me an opening to end the confrontation peacefully. My crew had the restraint and skill to neutralize most situations before they even started.

But not always.

There were times I had to use my jiu-jitsu. Not to hurt, but to control. Usually, it was someone drunk, high, or both. When words failed, and they kept swinging, I did what I had to. If a wrist lock didn't work, I escalated. And yes, sometimes I had to put someone to 'sleep'.

I know how that sounds, but a choke, when done right, isn't violent. You cut the blood flow to the brain for a few seconds, and they go out. You let go, they wake up, confused but unharmed, and the fight's over.

One night, I had to take down a guy who was at least 6'7", pushing 300 pounds. He came at me wild. I slipped under, took his back, and went for the rear-naked choke. But he was too big, I couldn't finish it standing. So, I kicked his legs out, brought him down, sunk in the choke, and held tight. My coworker gave me the signal that he was out. We elevated his legs, got the blood flowing again, and just like that, he came to. He got up quietly and walked right out the door.

That's what skill can do. It ends the chaos without adding to it.

Now, don't get me wrong, there's a difference between size and fight. I've seen big, athletic guys, football players, hockey brawlers, try to throw down. But unless you've trained to fight, it's a whole different game. It's not about brute force. It's about being calm under pressure and knowing exactly what to do when everything goes sideways.

But even with training, one rule never changes: you always need backup.

I remember one night when a guy lost a pool game and snapped. He broke his cue stick and started swinging. We disarmed him, and I put him in a Sankyo wrist lock, a brutal Aikido move, and started walking him out. On the way, he looked at me and said, "Now it's your turn. I'm going to wait for you."

That could've been an empty threat, but we took it seriously. Later that night, a cab driver tipped us off. He was out in the parking lot, armed and waiting.

When he stepped through the front door again, my head of security grabbed him from behind. The gun hit the floor. He ran, jumped in his car, and took off. A local patrol officer picked him up not long after. I confirmed his identity without hesitation.

And what did he get? Only one night in jail. A slap on the wrist.

That night stuck with me.

Security isn't just about keeping a door. It's about reading people, de-escalating violence, and relying on a team that's got your back no matter what.

I loved that team. We built a brotherhood. And even though we weren't in a ring or cage, those nights at the club were some of the realest fights of our lives.

Smoke and Second Thoughts

There was just one thing I couldn't stand: the cigarette smoke. It reminded me of working in chemical plants. I'd come home, peel off my clothes in the laundry room, and scrub the stink off me in the shower. It wore on me.

One day, Susan told me she couldn't figure me out. She thought maybe I was in witness protection or a retired cop. I laughed. Who would I have thought if I'd met myself for the first time?

New Friends, New Business

My time at the club became the unexpected launchpad for the next phase of my life. I met hundreds of people each week, including yacht brokers and business owners. Many became friends and eventually, clients. I installed water systems in their homes, offices, and boats.

One install led to another, and soon, I had a small operation growing by word of mouth. I hadn't even picked a name yet, and everyone just started calling me *H2O Leo*. It stuck.

The Spark Returns

That second job helped us save for a new four-bedroom home. It gave me stability. It gave me the traction I needed to start building a life again with the dream of bringing my kids to Florida for good.

But I knew if I wanted to be the father they deserved, I couldn't keep working nights forever.

It was time to build something bigger. Something lasting. And it all started at a nightclub.

Pushing Hard for 44 Hours

When the call came, I didn't hesitate because bringing my kids home wasn't a choice; it was my calling.

And here's what happened next:

My former wife called me out of the blue and said, "If you're ready, come get the kids." She was struggling, and deep down, she knew they needed stability.

My heart raced with excitement, and I called my mom and dad right away. My dad, without hesitation, said, "I'll go with you."

We left the very next day and drove straight through to New Jersey. First stop: my lawyer's office, where I picked up the paperwork I needed. Then I dropped my dad off at my sister Cindy's house so he could get some sleep; he had earned it.

I had a mountain to move in one day. I needed my former wife to sign paperwork with a notary. My lawyer's notary offered to help, so I brought her with me to my ex's workplace in Delaware. We signed and notarized everything, and it was now official. Then I raced straight to the courthouse to file the paperwork so I could legally take my kids back to Florida.

It took all day, but I got it done. That evening, we packed my kids' things into the back of the truck, scooped up my dad, and started the long journey back home. I had already been up for about 36 hours, but my adrenaline and sheer will to get my kids home kept me pushing through for 44. My dad urged me to sleep, but I said, "No way! I'm getting as far from Jersey as I can."

Since his eyesight was affected by macular degeneration, he couldn't help with the drive; it was all me. We made it as far as South Carolina before finally stopping at a motel. I crashed for ten straight hours. When I woke up, I had my kids, my dad, and a heart full of purpose. I was a father on a mission.

Back in Florida, I knew it was time to level up. It was time to grow my water business, not just for me, but for them. My kids were with me now, and I had a family to build around.

Puddles, Pirates, and a Proposal

Having my children with me in Florida felt like the final piece of my heart had come home. Life was giving me a second chance, not just at fatherhood, but at love, family, and something real.

LeAnn was a light in our lives. After everything I'd been through, heartbreak, rebuilding, loss, she brought joy and calm that lifted us all. She loved my kids like they were her own. As a mother of two, she knew what it meant to care deeply and to start again. She understood my journey because she was living a version of her own.

It felt effortless and natural. Our lives just clicked. We weren't perfect, but together, we were better. So, one weekend, I decided to take a family trip to Key West. Just me, LeAnn, and the kids, five hours south to a place of laid-back energy, tropical vibes, and unforgettable fun.

We had lunch at the Hard Rock and were walking down Duval Street when it started to pour. Most people would have run for cover. Not LeAnn. She and the kids started dancing and splashing in the puddles as if it were the best thing that had ever happened. They laughed, spun in circles, soaked and smiling.

I stood back and watched, completely in awe. "Look at her," I thought, "Look at them. She's not just happy, she brings happiness. To them. To me."

That's when I saw a pirate costume shop near the docks. Just beyond it was an old schooner named The Liberty. Something sparked inside me. I imagined us coming back, all dressed up like pirates, sailing the sea as a family.

And just like that, I knew.

LeAnn wasn't just someone I loved; she was it. The one. My future. My forever.

I didn't have a ring or a plan, but I had the moment. That night, after the kids were asleep, we sat on the patio of our hotel room, overlooking the pool and tiki bar, the warm Key West breeze carrying the sound of distant music.

I looked at her and said, "What do you think about coming back to the Keys... doing something wild... renting a tall ship, dressing up like pirates, and making us official?"

She looked at me, wide-eyed, trying to read my face. Then tears welled up in her eyes, and she asked, "Are you asking me to marry you?"

And just like that, I was the one who said Yes!

We got married in Key West on November 15, 2003.

I somehow ended up taking on the role of wedding planner, yes, me! But with LeAnn by my side, we made it happen together, piece by piece. We invited friends and family, not knowing who could actually make it. Life, of course, threw us a few curveballs.

LeAnn was dealing with some tough family challenges, and then my sister needed emergency surgery. My parents stayed back to be with her. Then two of my closest childhood friends dropped out. Jimmy L. fell down a flight of stairs and broke his back, and Lewis, my best friend from New Jersey, the one who was supposed to be my best man, had to stay behind when his son got into some serious trouble.

It felt like everyone was falling away, one by one. I started to wonder if maybe we should pause the whole thing. Maybe it wasn't the right time.

But every single person we spoke to said the same thing: **"Keep going. Get married."**

That's when my friend Mark stepped in right when I needed someone most. We met while working on a yacht in West Palm Beach, two guys thrown together by chance and saltwater. What started as small talk on the deck turned into a solid friendship built on trust, long hours, and a shared sense of humor. When Lewis couldn't be there, Mark didn't hesitate. He stepped up not just as a coworker but as a true friend.

Despite everything, I am happy we went ahead with the wedding. Our hearts were full, and our families, however scattered, were cheering us on. We gathered a crew of people who mattered most, and the schooner, originally seeming too big, ended up being just right.

My brother Steven, his wife, my Aunt Rose (my godmother), and Uncle Rick stood in for my parents. Aunt Rose and Uncle Rick had always inspired me with their joy, generosity, and the way they cared for family. I've always tried to carry that spirit with me.

We had our pre-wedding bash at Fat Tuesday. It was wild and unforgettable. The bar owner loved us so much that he offered to keep the party going just for us. Our nightclub crew showed up. Even Sue, the club manager, sent two cases of champagne since she couldn't be there in person.

The morning of the big day, we put on our pirate costumes, me as Captain Morgan, LeAnn as a stunning wench, and paraded down the dock. Tourists thought we were some kind of community festival. It felt like a fairy tale.

A local official married us on the deck of the schooner as it sailed south. The sun was setting, the sea calm, the air full of salt and laughter. At one point, a speedboat approached. We all turned to look. It was the owner of Fat Tuesday also in pirate gear, bowing and shouting, "Permission to come aboard, Captain."

We laughed until our sides hurt.

We held our reception at the Hard Rock, then partied deep into the night at Fat Tuesday. Our guests stayed for several days. It was magical. A celebration of love, new beginnings, and the beauty of unexpected joy.

We started a tradition that day, one we've kept for 20 years. Every year, we return to Key West to celebrate our anniversary. We missed only once, in 2021, due to the pandemic and family illness. But in 2022, we were back, and we plan to keep going as long as the ocean calls.

Because that's what love is. Not just the wedding, not just the party. It's puddles, pirates, and proposals. It's showing up, again and again, and choosing joy.

Every single year.

From miles on the road to deep changes in the heart, I fought through exhaustion to bring my kids home, driven by pure love and the will to give them the life they deserved. I rebuilt not just my business, but a sense of home, trust, and purpose.

LeAnn came into our lives like a breath of fresh air; her joy, her strength, and her love completed the family I was trying to hold together. Together, we found magic in everyday moments: rain puddles, late-night talks, and a Key West pirate wedding that brought laughter and unity to our lives.

It was chaotic. It was beautiful. And it was real.

This was more than just a fresh start; it was the moment when everything began to fall into place, when love, family, and purpose all found their way home.

Chapter 15:
Rebuilding More Than Homes

Every Cloud Has a Silver Lining

It was 2004 when I first met Pete at the nightclub I was managing. The owner had big plans to remodel and brought Pete in as the contractor. From the start, we clicked because he was a builder, and I was a plumber with hands-on experience constructing homes. Naturally, we teamed up for the club renovations. Then came the storm.

A major hurricane, a Category 4, was barreling toward the Treasure Coast. Forecasts warned of 156 mph winds with even stronger gusts. It was the kind of storm that leaves scars.

I called Pete and asked if he had any plywood to cover the club windows. He had plenty and offered to sell them to me for $20 a sheet.

I took what I needed for the club, but pretty soon, other local business owners started asking if we could board up their storefronts too. That's when the entrepreneur in me kicked in.

We bought all of Pete's plywood and hit the streets with help from the nightclub's doormen, whom we called the muscle. We hustled all day across town, boarding up offices, restaurants, homes, anything and everything.

The hurricane hit hard, and power was out for nearly two weeks. When the dust settled, Pete and I met up again to square away the payment for about 100 sheets of plywood.

But by then, we both knew we had something bigger here. We could do so much more.

Pete knew the cleanup effort was going to be massive. He told me straight up, "I'm going to need help to keep up with all the repair work through my contracting company." Then he asked me to come work with him, helping to restore the homes damaged by the storm.

I didn't hesitate.

I knew this was an opportunity not just to rebuild homes, but to rebuild something for my own family. A real chance to grow, to move forward. I couldn't miss it.

The Second Leap

After two years working on boats and managing the nightclub, I made a bold decision. It was time to bet on myself again. I chose to leave both jobs and go work with Pete while rebuilding my water business from the ground up. It was a huge risk. I had a family to support, bills to pay, and the fear of failure hanging over me like a storm cloud. But something deep inside told me it was time.

When I gave my notice to the marine company, I expected resistance. Instead, the owner called me from the Fort Lauderdale office and caught me off guard. He didn't try to convince me to stay. Instead, he said, "If you still want to sell and install water makers, I'll sell you everything you need at wholesale prices." He told me I was the first employee who truly understood water systems, and he didn't want to lose the momentum we had built together. That vote of confidence meant more than he probably realized. It gave me a solid foundation to stand on as I stepped into the unknown.

I dove in headfirst. I started attending every boat show across Florida, reconnecting with brokers and builders, striking up new conversations, chasing every lead. Slowly but surely, opportunities came in, installing water makers on some of the most beautiful yachts in the world. But it didn't stop there. Captains, engineers, and yacht owners began asking for systems in their homes and businesses, too. What started as marine work turned into full-spectrum water filtration. Some of those early clients became lifelong friends.

Momentum was back on my side.

But there was still one more chapter to close: The nightclub. As much as I had grown there, I knew I couldn't work nights anymore. My kids needed me at home. One day after a team meeting, I stayed behind and sat down with Sue, the owner. I told her it was time. She understood, but I could tell it stung a bit. Later, one of the DJs pulled me aside and said, "You're the first manager here who has ever quit. All the others were fired." That stuck with me.

I walked away on my own terms, with my dignity, my vision, and a second chance.

Flipping Homes

Besides repairing roofs and fixing water damage after the storm, Pete and I stayed busy with projects for nearly a year. We kept the momentum going, but we also started discussing the next major move. Pete had an idea to buy damaged homes, renovate them, and resell them for a profit.

I was all in.

With my experience and having built my own home, the one we affectionately called The Itchy Foot, I knew what it took to get the job done right. We bought four houses, rolled up our sleeves, and got to work.

LeAnn stepped in, too, handling the sales side through For Sale By Owner. She was sharp, resourceful, and knew how to present a home in its best light. Together, we made a great team, hustling hard, turning homes around, and watching the fruits of our labor pay off.

But just as we sold the last house, the Florida real estate market came crashing down. Hard.

Riding the Crash

When the housing market collapsed, it felt like the floor dropped out from under us. One minute, we were making solid returns on the homes we'd just poured our hearts and energy into, then suddenly, buyers vanished, lending froze, and prices plummeted.

Pete and I were fortunate in some ways. We had sold our last house just before the real crash hit, but the impact still rippled through everything. Work slowed down, people were scared to spend money, and contractors were scrambling just to stay afloat. For many, it was a time of panic.

But I had been through storms before. Real ones. Financial ones. Emotional ones. And I wasn't about to give up now.

Instead of folding, I shifted gears. I leaned into what I knew best: clean water. The one thing every home still needed, crash or no crash, was safe, healthy water. And people were starting to wake up to what was really in their taps.

The housing market was in freefall, but I saw an opportunity. While others were focused on flipping houses or scraping by on repairs, I doubled down on water purification education, installation, and building trust one home at a time.

It wasn't flashy, but it was steady. Honest work. And slowly, things began to turn.

Water, Wealth, and Times Square

Pete and Me in NYC

Even after the housing market crashed, the three of us, Pete, LeAnn, and I, weren't done building something together. We worked well as a team, and I had a new idea that could be big.

I pitched Pete on a new concept: water coolers. But not just the standard ones with 5-gallon jugs. I told him to think of them like rental properties, each one bringing in steady monthly income. He was all ears. Pete already owned several real estate investments, so the idea of generating recurring revenue with coolers made sense to him.

I'd been keeping an eye on how fast water cooler businesses were growing in New Jersey and Delaware. I knew this was our shot at doing something even better in Florida.

At that time, I was a member of a water technology trade association. One day, I saw an ad in their industry magazine:

a national company was looking for new dealers across the country. I didn't waste a second and called to say, "I want Florida. All of it."

Next thing you know, Pete, LeAnn, and I went on a road trip to Delaware to meet with the VP of the company. The meeting went great. We signed on the spot and secured the rights to become the exclusive dealer in Florida.

While we were up north finalizing the deal, I brought Pete to my hometown in New Jersey, just 20 minutes from the office. I took him to The Itchy Foot, the house I had built with my own hands. No one was living there at the time, so we walked the property. Pete took it all in and said, "This is spectacular."

That meant a lot. That house had been more than just a home. It was a symbol of everything I'd built and lost. But now, standing there with Pete, I felt a sense of closure. I was in a better place. Physically. Emotionally. Financially.

We stayed up north for a few extra days. Spent time with family. Boated with my old friend Jimmy L. We cracked open piles of blue claw crabs. It brought back a flood of memories from the river days.

Then we headed to New York to visit Pete's family. They welcomed us with open arms and full plates. One night, we went into Manhattan and saw Dirty Rotten Scoundrels on Broadway. John Lithgow had us in stitches.

After the show, we grabbed drinks in Times Square. We talked about everything: the business, the brand, the future. That's when Pete raised his glass and said, "This is a no-brainer."

We all laughed. That was it. The name stuck. No Brainer, LLC was born.

Back in Florida, we hit the ground running. We began leasing and installing water coolers in offices, hospitals, and medical practices. These weren't your typical bottled coolers. Ours had a built-in reverse osmosis system that provides cleaner, safer, and better-tasting water without the need for lifting 45-pound jugs or worrying about bacteria in plastic bottles.

No bottles. No hassle. Just pure water on demand.

Within three years, we were named Dealer of the Year three times in a row. We were leasing more coolers than any other distributor in the country.

As demand grew, so did our offerings. Clients started asking for coffee service, so we launched Cooler Beans, one of the first authorized Keurig dealers in South Florida. We eventually expanded into espresso and cappuccino machines, especially popular with the Latin community.

But as with any business, change is inevitable.

Ownership shifted at the water cooler franchise. The split was amicable, and we divided the contracts and retained our top accounts. Many of those clients are still with us today.

But we didn't slow down. We evolved.

We have introduced our own proprietary systems, and now, with our special filtration system, we are bringing antioxidant-rich, pH-balanced water to homes and businesses throughout Florida.

We had water systems in hospitals, executive offices, and luxury homes. We were finally standing on a solid foundation.

But just as everything seemed to be coming together, life was about to throw me another curveball.

* The ideas and information shared here are not medical advice—please check with your healthcare provider before making changes to your healthcare routine.

Chapter 16:
Love Brought Me Back

Surviving a Near-Death Experience

Within a few years, I was officially back in business. Things were finally moving quickly again and full of promise. For a moment, I thought I had outrun the pain of the past, thought maybe, just maybe, life was finally giving me a break.

But just as the light began to shine again, the darkness came crashing in.

It started with subtle whispers from my body that something was off. I ignored them. I was approaching 40 and chalked it up to stress. I had too much to build, too many people depending on me. I kept pushing. I thought once the business was stabilized, everything would settle down.

But I was wrong.

My heart began to betray me. It didn't just race; it roared. Sometimes, it would pound over 200 beats per minute, like it was trying to break free from my chest. Doctors couldn't give me answers. They gave me pills to "calm" me, but they dulled my senses instead. I felt sedated, hollowed out, like a shadow of myself. The fire that fueled my ambition, the purpose that drove me, flickered to almost nothing.

Then one afternoon, everything came crashing down.

I was playing with my daughter Nadine, laughing, chasing her through the house. It was just a regular, beautiful moment... until my chest clenched tight. My legs buckled. The floor rushed up to meet me. My heart exploded into chaos, hitting 280 bpm.

I collapsed.

Leo Junior, just a kid, had to call 911. I remember hearing the panic in his voice before everything blurred. EMTs arrived fast, but nothing they did could pull me back.

My wife was out of state visiting family. I felt completely alone. I wasn't thinking about the business. I wasn't thinking about money.

I was thinking about dying.

And not just dying, I was terrified I'd die in front of my kids. The thought of that was almost worse than the pain I was experiencing.

Pete, my friend and business partner, raced to the ER. The doctors tried everything. Nothing worked. They hit me with shock after shock, trying to pull me out of atrial fibrillation.

Nothing.

I remember the heat rising in my chest, like my soul was trying to claw its way out. A crushing weight pressed down on me. My vision tunneled.

And then... silence.

I flatlined. No pulse. No breath. No sound. Just darkness. For over a minute, I was gone.

People always ask, "Did you see anything?"

And the truth is… I did.

I was somewhere else. Bright. Still. Peaceful. I couldn't see faces, but I knew I wasn't alone. I felt surrounded by warmth, by love, like my grandfather was there, or maybe all those I'd lost. There was no fear. No pain. Just a still, surreal comfort. I would have been happy to stay, not afraid.

And then I snapped back to reality.

I woke up strapped to a table, drenched in sweat, heart pounding, fists clenched like I was in a fight. Pete was standing next to me, pale and wrecked, his voice trembling:

"Don't you dare die on me again."

He later told me that when the adrenaline hit my chest and kicked my heart back into rhythm, I shot off the table like a man possessed. I ripped out wires, jumped up swinging, yelling, "Who hit me!" A security guard and a couple of nurses had to strap me back down.

The fighter in me had never left. When I came to again and saw that the heart monitor was reading steadily at 80 bpm, I broke down inside. I was alive. I wasn't supposed to be, but I was. I had been given another chance. Another breath. Another day to be a father.

They kept me in the hospital for ten long days. My heart was bruised, and they worried about clots. Test after test. Blood draws. CT scans. Meds that made me nauseous and dizzy. My body was a battlefield.

A friend in the pharmaceutical world helped me get switched to gentler medications, which helped, but I still felt like I was walking on the edge.

Eventually, the cardiologist came in with news that felt like a riddle.

"It's not your heart," he said. "It's the wiring around it. Think of your heart like a perfect engine, but the wires are crossed."

That metaphor hit a little too close to home.

I wanted to believe that was the end of it. But it wasn't.

The fear stayed. It settled in like an unwelcome tenant. I became hypersensitive to everything: smells, foods, light, and sound. Panic attacks would hit me out of nowhere. I couldn't drive. Couldn't go outside. Could barely leave the couch.

LeAnn bought me a recliner so I could sleep downstairs. I couldn't bear the thought of dying alone in the night, and out of reach. I started calling it my "death chair." I said it half-jokingly, but inside, I meant it.

I felt trapped in my own body. Broken. Haunted.

Hunted by the possibility that the next attack would be the one that took me for good.

And even now, when I look back at that time... I still can't believe I made it through.

Those were dark days indeed.

In that one minute when my heart stopped, my whole world reset. Everything that used to seem urgent: deadlines, sales, and arguments, vanished. What remained was crystal clear: love, family, life.

I wasn't just brought back by a shock or adrenaline; I believe I was pulled back by love. The love of my kids. Of Pete, standing beside me. Of LeAnn, who never gave up on me.

The truth is, I wasn't just reborn, I was forged again.

And in those seconds of stillness on the other side, I felt it. A deep knowing that life is a gift, not a guarantee. I carry that forward now not as fear, but as fire. I came back for a reason. And I intend to live like it.

A Second Chance Beats Stronger

I was only 40 when I suffered a major heart attack. It was a wake-up call, sudden, terrifying, and impossible to ignore. One minute, I was chasing my daughter through the house, and the next, I was on the floor, heart racing out of control, the world spinning around me.

That moment flatlining, facing the edge, changed everything.

I used to think strength meant powering through, never slowing down, always staying tough. But real strength came when I was strapped to that table, terrified, vulnerable, and still choosing to come back. Not for pride. Not for ego. But for love of my kids, my wife, and my family.

I don't know why I came back when so many don't. But I do know this: every beat of my heart now feels like a gift. Every sunrise, every laugh, every hug from my children, none of it is taken for granted.

* The ideas and information shared here are not medical advice—please check with your healthcare provider before making changes to your healthcare routine.

Chapter 17:
Why Am I Still Here?

There was a time when I couldn't answer that question.

After the school shooting, my life felt like a string of close calls. I somehow managed to walk away from explosions at chemical plants. Slipped and nearly fell from seventy feet in the air. Came within inches from getting shot three times: once at school, once during a water system installation, once working security at a club, and then came the day I flatlined in a hospital bed.

More than once, I looked up at the sky and asked, ***"Why am I still here?"***

I realized I must have a purpose, and someone or something bigger than me must've been watching out. That's the only explanation I've got.

In the aftermath of that last near-death experience, I didn't recover. I just floated along. Lost in a medicated fog, I was drained physically, emotionally, and spiritually. I couldn't connect with my family, my work, or even myself. Every day felt like a struggle for survival and not a life worth living.

Then one morning, something shifted.

I didn't just open my eyes; I *woke up*. For the first time in what felt like forever, I saw through the haze. It was as if something inside me had been rebooted. A faint spark lit up. Not enough to run a marathon, but enough to remind me I was still alive.

I sat on the edge of the bed, looked around, and realized I had a choice: either stay stuck in survival mode or fight my way back.

And deep down, I knew I hadn't been spared all those times just to fade away.

If I wanted to be there for my kids… if I wanted to rebuild my life… I couldn't leave it all in the hands of pills and prescriptions. I had to take control of my own health.

And so, I began to search not just for answers, but for solutions.

That brush with death forced me to look deeper. To question everything.

That shift in mindset sparked a mission. I dove deep into the science behind water, the heart, and the body. I researched how hydration affects energy, healing, and cardiovascular function. I spent years developing a new type of filtration system. I could stand behind one that did it all, one I would trust with my own family.

Water, Voltage, and the Will to Live

That's when I discovered something that changed everything: the body needs voltage to heal. Literally, every organ operates on electrical potential, and none more so than the heart. I knew this intimately as I'd rewired homes, fixed engines, and installed entire water treatment plants. I understood the importance of proper wiring and charge.

According to research I uncovered, particularly from **Dr. Jerry Tennant's groundbreaking book Healing Is**

Voltage, "the heart requires strong voltage to function at its best."[1]

---

[1] **Dr. Jerry Tennant, MD – Tennant Institute**
www.tennantinstitute.com

That's when water entered the picture again, but not in the way I had known it before.

I had spent my entire career dealing with water in every form imaginable, rusty wells, sewer lines, desalinators, and medical-grade purification for dialysis machines. But never before had I asked the question: *Can water actually heal us?*

Steven G

That's when I met a great guy with whom I was working on a project at the time. Down-to-earth, curious, and full of good energy. He had recently started using alkaline, negatively charged water that had helped his wife recover from a serious health issue. Steven could see I wasn't doing well myself and, knowing I worked with water, thought I might be interested in trying it.

At first, I shrugged it off; I was being the skeptical, hard-headed Jersey plumber that I am. But Steven didn't give up on me. He brought me gallons of that water to test and said, "Just check the numbers. You'll know if it's legit."

And sure enough... the numbers looked good. No red flags. But what surprised me most?

It didn't trigger my A-Fib.

Everything else did; calcium, fluoride, even toothpaste would send my heart into chaos. But this water? It gave me energy. Focus. Calm. For the first time in months, I felt a glimmer of hope.

Steven never tried to sell me anything. He just shared what worked for his wife and gently encouraged me to look deeper. That kind of support without ego or agenda meant a lot. He didn't just offer water; he offered me a new path forward.

Looking back now, I know it wasn't a coincidence that we crossed paths. Steven was a messenger, one of those rare people who show up in your life exactly when you need them.

And from that moment on, everything started to change.

The more I studied, the deeper I delved. I was told that when water is structured correctly down to micro or nano-clusters, it hydrates more efficiently and carries more than just H_2O. It carries electrons. It can act like an antioxidant, reducing free radicals and oxidative stress. I would find out that it was more than that, the true healing powers came from DH (Dissolved Hydrogen), better known as Molecular Hydrogen.[2]

That was the missing link.

---

[2] **Hydrogen Water Research**
www.molecularhydrogeninstitute.org

So, I dove in literally and figuratively. I tested mineral blends, tracked ORP (oxidation-reduction potential), and experimented with many types of water systems. I spent thousands of dollars on equipment and rare gemstones and minerals, trying to find the perfect 'charge'.

Most didn't work. But I would find one that did.

Then came the (WQA) Water Quality Association Conference in Las Vegas. I wasn't feeling great. Truthfully, I didn't want to go but LeAnn had planned the trip, and I said yes for her sake. Turns out, it was exactly where I needed to be.

Divine Timing, Determined Heart

That morning, I attended the WQA trade show and experienced an A-Fib episode just walking the floor. No water was in sight, even at a water convention. I chewed my meds dry and sat down on a bench, feeling completely wrecked. That's when a Korean scientist took the stage just feet in front of me.

He began speaking about energized water and voltage. My ears perked up.

His words, though spoken in broken English, matched everything I'd been researching. He spoke about how much voltage the heart needed to function, how water could carry that energy.

How structured, mineralized, and hydrogen-rich water could deliver healing at a cellular level.

It felt like divine timing.

After the talk, my heart finally stabilized. I found the strength to get up, grabbed a bottle of water, washed the taste of my heart meds from my mouth, and headed straight to his booth. With help from his daughter, who translated, he explained his mineral blend and even gave me samples to take home.

That trip changed everything.

Back to Basics: Clean, Healthy, and Revolutionary

What I created was cleaner, healthier, and, believe it or not, less expensive than most of the high-end water systems on the market.
But to get there, I had to strip everything back. I had to return to the core idea:
Pure, functional water energized the way nature intended.
No more metal plates. No electricity.
The real charge, the one the body craves, comes from **minerals**, the kind our ancestors got from natural spring water.
So, I designed a system that first **purifies** the water, then reintroduces healthy, bioavailable minerals in just the right ratios to mimic nature's blueprint.
Compact. Affordable. Powerful.
And then came the hydrogen, that beautiful, elusive molecule: H_2.
It acts like an antioxidant, neutralizing free radicals and fueling the body with cellular energy.[3]
But it wasn't enough to just create hydrogen. I had to figure out how to **store** it under pressure, so it stayed dissolved in the water until the very moment it hit your glass.
I built my first prototype. It wasn't pretty; it broke filter housings with too much hydrogen gas. But we refined it, added a pressure-release system, and finally created

[3] **Hydrogen Water Research**
www.molecularhydrogeninstitute.org

something stable. That's when I knew we were onto something.

I called it "Healthified Water," water that didn't just hydrate but supported healing on a cellular level.

To prove it, I tested it on myself.

I drank nearly two gallons a day. And within weeks, the man who once couldn't walk up a flight of stairs without fear... was running.

No toxins.

No gimmicks.

Just **results**.

It wasn't easy. It took time, resources, and relentless persistence.

But once I got it right, I knew we had something **revolutionary**.

Now, we've got clients all over the country who won't drink anything else.

We've created what I lovingly call a generation of **"water snobs,"** people whose bodies have learned the difference between average hydration and the kind that **energizes every cell**.

Arlo Guthrie and me

One of my favorite stories comes from the folk singer **Arlo Guthrie**.

After we installed his new system, he poured his first glass and drank it down. A few minutes later, he looked at me and said,

"Leo, why am I still thirsty?"

I smiled and told him the truth.

"That's your body talking. You've been dehydrated at the **cellular level** for years. Now you're finally giving it what it needs."

A few days later, Arlo called me.

"You were right," he said. "I feel incredible. This water hits differently. I didn't realize how thirsty I was until I wasn't anymore."

That's what this water does.

It doesn't just **quench thirst;** it repairs damage.

And that's why one of my favorite sayings will always be true:

An ounce of prevention is worth a pound of cure.

"Necessity is the Mother of all Inventions."

I was walking again. Then jogging. Then running. It felt surreal.

Normally, exercise like that would send my heart rate into a chaotic state. But something had changed. The water, the healing, and the mindset. It was all starting to work.

One afternoon, Leo Jr. and I were out for a walk around the neighborhood. As we neared the last block, something inside me stirred something I hadn't felt in a long time.

Freedom.

I looked over at my son... then I took off sprinting.

It felt like a scene out of Forrest Gump, like I was breaking through invisible braces I didn't even know were still holding me back. In my head, I heard it:

"Run, Leo, run!"

Leo Jr. chased after me, shouting at me to stop. He was scared, and I understood why. He had seen what I'd been through. He knew the warnings, the fear, the heart.

But at that moment, I wasn't afraid.

I ran hard and fast all the way to the front door.

When we got home, Leo Jr. ran straight to

LeAnn and told her what had happened. She looked at me, stunned, and placed her hand on my chest.

She counted the beats. One by one. Eighty.

Steady.

Strong.

Her eyes went wide with shock and something else, hope.

The doctors had said I'd never run again. But I just had.

And I felt alive.

Healing, Purpose, and Power in Every Drop!

Water, my healthified water, gave me my life back.

It gave me my heart, my strength, my family, and my future.

I wasn't broken anymore.

I walked straight into the living room, picked up the so-called "death chair" LeAnn had bought me, and carried it right out to the curb. The truth is, it was a nice chair, expensive even, but I hated what it stood for. There was a time in my life when I honestly believed I might die in that chair. It had become a symbol of giving up, of waiting for the end.

LeAnn told me someone picked it up within minutes of me putting it out there. I'm sure whoever took it saw it for what it really was, a comfortable place to sit. But for me, it was a coffin with cushions. And I was done with it.

This journey taught me that healing is possible when you combine knowledge, purpose, and belief. That even in the darkest moments, we can find something worth fighting for. And for me, that something was more than survival; it was transformation.

I didn't just discover a new business. I found a mission. Now, I help others the way I once needed help myself by showing them that the right water isn't just clean. It's powerful.

It's healing.

It's hope.

It's life.

Looking back, I see more than recovery; I see resurrection.

What nearly took me out became the very fuel that ignited a new fire within me. I didn't just survive, I woke up. Woke up to a deeper understanding of the human body, the power of belief, and the profound role water plays in our health and healing.

It wasn't just about fixing my heart; it was about finding my purpose.

From dirty basements and crawl spaces to skyscrapers and mega yachts, I had worked with water in almost every imaginable way. But it wasn't until I came face-to-face with death that I realized water isn't just something we drink, it's something that can save us. Charge us. Restore us. That realization turned into a mission.

And now, every time I help someone find healing through healthy water, I feel that same voltage run through me again. I'm not just helping people filter their water, I'm helping them rewrite their story.

And if mine is proof of anything, it's this: It's never too late to come back stronger.

The ideas and information shared here are not medical advice—please check with your healthcare provider before making changes to your healthcare routine.

Chapter 18:
"Rewired by Water"

How I Discovered the Healing Power of Water

By the time I reached my early 40s, I had lived through enough for a few lifetimes working in toxic chemical plants, battling heart problems, enduring a near-death experience, and clawing my way back to health. Through it all, one element followed me: water.

Not just clean water. Not just safe water. I was searching for something more: Water that could heal.

That journey started years earlier with the pain and uncertainty of a body that had betrayed me. After collapsing in front of my children, flatlining in the hospital, and being revived, I knew I had been given a second chance.

One day, at a concert in West Palm Beach, I entered a pull-up contest run by Army recruiters. After doing twenty pull-ups, I won a shirt. The recruiter asked if I wanted to enlist. I told him I was 42. He thought I was much younger. I laughed and said, "It's the water."

The final proof came about 8 years later when I decided to apply for my pilot's license. I had completed 20 hours of flight school before it was time for my solo flight, but the FAA had denied me because of my past medical history. I went back to my old cardiologist, Dr. B, whom I had not seen in years. He thought I was either dead or with a new doctor.

When he saw me fit, full of energy, and thriving, he couldn't believe it. He ran every test in the book: stress tests, echocardiograms, even a month-long heart monitor. I passed them all. Then he looked at me and asked, "How did you do it?"

At first, I hesitated. "I'm not sure you'll believe me," I said. "Try me," he replied.

So, I did. I told him about my water, about the minerals, the hydrogen, and the negative charge. I braced for the usual eye roll or polite nod. But it never came.

He didn't laugh. He didn't dismiss it. He listened.

I felt truly heard. A modern medical doctor was actually taking me seriously. I was excited. Energized. Validated. After everything I'd been through, that moment meant more than I can explain.

Then he said, "Hook one of your systems up in my office. I want to try it."

We've since installed our systems in all his offices, and he told me it helped with his heartburn. And that's a start.

My journey from collapse to recovery wasn't easy. But it gave me purpose.

Clean water isn't enough anymore. People need healthy water. Water that nourishes and protects.

And I've made it my life's mission to give it to them.

Water That Heals - Easier Said Than Done

Looking back, when I built the first version of my new type of water system, I was eager to share what it had done for me. I met with peers in the water treatment industry, excited to explain how this new kind of water had changed my life, how it supported my recovery, helped my heart, and given me back my energy. However, instead of encouragement, I faced resistance.

A lot of it.

Many of these guys had known me for years. They had built systems, fought water quality battles, and seen what I'd seen. But the idea that I could change the structure of water, charge it with electrons, give it antioxidant power, and affect the body on a cellular level, they laughed. Literally.

I found it easy to swallow… because I drank it every day. (LOL)

But deep down, I knew their doubt came from the same place mine had once lived in uncertainty. I was once the hard-headed Jersey plumber who wouldn't believe any of this either. Until I lived it.

Later on, some of those same skeptics came back around. A few recognized what we were doing and wanted to be part of it by adding our filtration technology to their own systems or even asking to work with us. I welcomed them with open arms. I have always been passionate about educating anyone who wants to learn more about healthy water.

Still, when I told others suffering from health issues, especially heart conditions like mine, that water had played a role in my recovery, they hesitated. It sounded too good to be true. Some were flat-out scared of it, like this water was "too different" to trust.

But how could I convince them?

I had seen the transformation in my own body. I understood what had caused my health issues, and I knew this "healthified" water was where it all turned around. I wanted to shout it from the rooftops. I wanted to tell the world: "Start with water. It's where healing begins."

I decided the best way to prove it was to stop selling it and start giving it away.

I gave my drinking systems to people who needed them most for free. Some were friends, while others were strangers I met in doctors' waiting rooms or through mutual acquaintances. Most of them tried it out because, well, why not? What did they have to lose?

Nearly all of them are still using our systems today. That's what matters.

But I knew this wouldn't reach the masses unless I could bridge the gap to the medical community. I needed real doctors to listen. I needed proof. I had no idea at the time that so many doctors even existed.

The first was Dr. Tennant, a brilliant physician, innovator, and educator, who came to Florida to meet me. He wanted to understand what we could do with water. That meeting changed everything.

We became collaborators, both committed to helping others understand the vital role voltage, minerals, and hydration play in the body's ability to heal. I was honored to serve as a keynote speaker at many of his conferences in Texas and Arizona. Through those events, I met doctors, researchers, and health professionals from all over the world, many of whom to this day, still recommend our water filtration systems.

That moment, standing in front of rooms filled with doctors, sharing my story and showing them the science, felt surreal. I had once been the guy who couldn't walk up a flight of stairs. Now I was sharing a system that helped people feel alive again.

This wasn't just about clean water anymore. This was about healing.

This was about purpose.

And this... this was just the beginning.

The Water Within

To go from lying helpless in a chair I called my "death chair" to sprinting down the street with my son... to running businesses again, to speaking on stages with renowned doctors, it feels like a second life.

And in many ways, it is.

I didn't just recover. I was rebuilt, reconstructed from the inside out, starting with the simplest, most powerful element we all take for granted: water.

But not just any water.

Water that could carry voltage. Water that could act as an antioxidant. Water that could heal not because it was magical, but because it gave my body what it had been missing all along: a clean, safe, mineral-rich, electron-charged foundation.

This wasn't a miracle. It was chemistry. It was physics. It was persistence.

But more than that, it was a purpose.

What began as a desperate mission to save my own life became a calling. I had discovered a way to bring healing not only to myself, but also to others who had been told they'd never get better, never feel whole again. People who were out of options.

And I knew what I had to do: share it.

Not for the money. Not for the recognition. But because I had been given something, I rarely had a second chance... A chance to do the kind of work that matters.

I'm not claiming that water fixes everything. But it was where my healing journey began. It's where the fog began to lift. It's what gave me the strength to fight again.

And maybe, just maybe, it can do that for someone else, too. That's why I keep going.

Because if I could come back from the edge... maybe someone reading this will believe they can too.

You just have to take the first sip.

* The ideas and information shared here are not medical advice—please check with your healthcare provider before making changes to your healthcare routine.

Chapter 19:
Waves of Change

A Family's Journey Back to Joy

With my health restored and my roles as a father, husband, and business owner back in balance, it was finally time to bring joy and adventure into our lives again. After everything we had been through, we deserved it. Pete had become more than a business partner; he was family. And weekends started to revolve around what we loved most: being close to the water.

Funny how life works. The heart issues I battled didn't just impact me; they affected everyone around me. My kids had held it together and were thriving in school. They also trained five days a week in MMA (Mixed Martial Arts) and Jiu-Jitsu and were making good progress. LeAnn, with Pete by her side, helped keep the business running smoothly while I focused on healing. After years of stress, we were finally settling into a rhythm, and I wanted to make sure we had some real fun along the way.

One day, Leo Jr. and I were installing water coolers at a boat manufacturing facility in Vero Beach. In the back of the shop, half-covered in dust, sat a sleek 27-foot Italian Go-Fast boat, which was silver and gray, something like out of a movie. I couldn't stop staring. I asked Robert, the owner, if it was for sale. He said only eight of these boats were made as luxury tenders for mega yachts. One had gone to a movie producer for a James Bond-style film. And this one was the only other one in the country.

The boat had some damage, a cracked windshield, and scuffs along the side, but I saw past that; I saw potential. When Robert offered it to me for $10,000, I didn't hesitate. It was a risk, but I could feel it in my gut: this boat was meant for us.

I pulled together the cash and towed it home to Jensen Beach, where we had recently moved to better schools and a house with a pool. That move alone felt like a fresh start.

Once I got the boat home, I dropped in new batteries, opened the hatch, and couldn't believe my eyes: a nearly new 496 HO Mercury engine with only 42 hours on it. That motor alone was worth tens of thousands.

A few small repairs later, and we launched our maiden voyage.

And man, it was perfect.

We cruised everywhere from Palm Beach to Vero Beach, even down to the Keys. Weekends became filled with stops at sandbars, ocean swims, and unforgettable family memories. It wasn't just about the boat. It was about being together again, laughing again, living again.

That decision to buy the boat turned out to be one of the best moves we ever made. It gave us time, joy, and a whole new set of stories and memories.

A couple of years later, while anchored at Peanut Island in Palm Beach, we ran into some of our clients, Suzie and her husband, Cosmo. Cosmo, a proud Italian, was immediately obsessed with the boat. "What kind of boat is this?" he asked.

With a smirk, I said, "It's a Ferrari." I was joking, but his eyes went wide. He was sold.

Later that week, Cosmo called and asked if I'd consider selling it. After some back-and-forth, we agreed on $85,000. I had only paid $10,000 and invested a few thousand in repairs. The profit helped us build the business and move into a bigger home with more room for the kids. Sure, I missed the boat, but the joy it gave us, the adventures we shared, and the return it gave our family were priceless. I flipped more cars than I could count to get ahead, and although it was a boat, it was no different. It's the businessman in me, I guess.

Most people say the happiest days of owning a boat are the day you buy it and the day you sell it. For me, both days brought happiness, but for very different reasons.

Months later, we all went out to dinner, LeAnn and me, Suzie and Cosmo. After a couple of glasses of wine, Cosmo turned to me and said, "Alright, Leo, what'd you really pay for that boat?"

I laughed. "You don't want to know."

But Cosmo insisted. His Italian spirit wasn't about to let me off the hook.

So, I told him. "Ten grand... plus a few grand in repairs. Let's say maybe $15,000 total."

He stared at me. Then came the words I can't repeat in this book, but let's just say the word "mother" was involved.

I picked up the dinner tab that night.

We still laugh about it, and Cosmo still cuts my hair; he hasn't taken an ear off yet, so I think we're good.

One thing about me is that I'm *H2O Leo*. I'm either working with water, boating on it, or living near it. Water isn't just my business, it's my passion, my peace, and my purpose.

And that's exactly why I do all the above, because water gave me my life back.

And now, I'm using it to help others reclaim theirs.

* The ideas and information shared here are not medical advice—please check with your healthcare provider before making changes to your healthcare routine.

Chapter 20:
Beyond Clean

The Rise Of pH Prescription

After selling our boat and finding a new home by the shore, it felt like we were finally moving up. Our new place wasn't directly on the water, but it was close, just one house away. If you stood in the right spot, you could see the glimmer of water and hear the hum of boats passing by. Not bad for a kid from New Jersey who once dreamed of a life surrounded by water.

I used to imagine building a watchtower on top of the house, like the one I had back in Jersey overlooking the Delaware River. That view, the peace it brought, never left me. And while I never had time to add that feature here, life was too full to dwell on regrets. This house had everything we needed. Two stories, plenty of room, and a huge screened-in pool, which I could take care of myself, thanks to my 'brother', Mike Geyer in Mesa, AZ, at Exceptional Water Systems. No chemicals, of course not for *H2O Leo*, my pool ran on oxygen and ozone, providing clean, safe, and healthy water, just like the water systems I designed.

By now, our business was no longer just local; we had expanded across the country. Thanks to the wellness conferences I had been speaking at nationwide, the word was spreading. What started as a water treatment company became a mission, and I found myself on stage in front of hundreds of doctors and health professionals with more credentials behind their names than I could keep track of.[4]

---

[4] **pH Prescription LLC**
www.phprescription.com

I'll be honest, at first, I was nervous. A high school dropout with no formal business education, standing in front of MDs, DDSs, NDs, and PhDs. I could feel my knees shaking as I clicked through the first few PowerPoint slides. But then something happened.

They started asking questions. Real questions. And I had the answers not from textbooks, but from years in the trenches. I knew water. I knew how to make it safe. And now, I have learned how to make it healthy. Most of them didn't even know there was a difference.

That day, everything changed.

I realized I could use the influence of these medical and wellness experts. I got them to experience the water first. Let them feel the results. And when they did, they wanted to share it. Many joined us as affiliates, recommending our systems to their clients. It worked better than I ever imagined.

Our phones rang nonstop. People wanted to learn more. My staff learned by listening to me on calls and by watching my presentations. Even our installers could explain the benefits of the systems. We were building something bigger than I ever dreamed of, and my whole family was a part of it.

I've had the honor of sitting with health experts from all over the country. I've traveled to nearly every state, saw the beauty of this country coast to coast, and broke bread with some of the most successful and influential people in the world. We have clients from all walks of life, some very famous and well-known. But what matters most is the connection, the mission, the shared belief that real water can heal.

Looking back, every step, every job, every toxic plant I worked in, every fight I walked away from in a nightclub, even flatlining… it was all leading me here. I trained my whole life for this. My father always told my mom, "Leo's going to shine one day." Now I know, he was right.

The Birth of pH Prescription™

One pivotal moment came when Dr. Jerry Tennant called me.[5]

Me and Dr Tennant

He needed three of our drinking systems fast. I wasn't producing them yet, so I scrambled to order the parts. When he followed up personally, wanting an ETA on the systems, I was not sure who he was. Just introducing himself as

[5] **Dr. Jerry Tennant, MD – Tennant Institute**
www.tennantinstitute.com

"Jerry," I was caught off guard. Then he said, "Jerry Tennant," he said. That got my attention. I knew him as Dr. Tennant.

I hurried to build the systems and shipped them out that Friday. I didn't even charge him yet. I wanted to make sure he and his team liked them first.

And they did.

He kept trying to pay me, but I held off until I got real feedback. When it came, it was unanimous: they loved the taste, the feel, the results. The body knows good water. And this... *was good water*.

We knew we needed a name for this new level of water technology, something that captured the essence of what we were doing. After weeks of brainstorming, we landed on it:

pH Prescription™ *Water Doctors Recommend*™

The name said it all.

We were altering the pH, infusing water with molecular hydrogen and trace minerals. It was not just clean, it was safe, healthy, functional, and powerful. And now, doctors are prescribing it to their patients.

Most people don't even realize that "pH" stands for Potential Hydrogen. But once they experienced our water, they understood the difference.

We secured the domain, built the website, and launched a full product line. It started with the water coolers we had been installing for years, then expanded to our new Healthy

Drinking Systems. From there, we added whole-home systems designed to protect families not just from what's in their drinking water, but from the toxins that come through their showers and baths.

We took the same technology we had once used to clean up toxic wells and refined it for modern, everyday living.

And people loved it.

From skeptical industry peers who once laughed at the idea of "antioxidant water," to doctors who now drink it daily and recommend it proudly, the tides are turning. They saw the science. They saw the results. And most of all, they saw the heart behind it.

We weren't just building a business. We were building a movement.

Why pH Prescription Exists

My Sunshine Nadine

We don't just purify water, we bring it back to life.

Water used to come from deep springs, full of minerals and natural antioxidants. Today, our tap water is filled with microplastics, PFAS, heavy metals, and other toxins that slowly destroy our health.

Most systems just superficially filter water. We go further.

At pH Prescription, we restore what was lost. After finely filtered purification, we add back the essential minerals, molecular hydrogen, and natural antioxidants that make water *truly healthy*.

Because clean water isn't enough.

Water should heal. Water should energize.

That's why we exist:
For health.
For meaning.
For life.

From Blueprints to Breakthroughs

Looking back, I see more than just the growth of a business. I see my growth as a person, as a father, and a husband who has a mission. I didn't set out to become a health advocate or speak in front of doctors. I set out to fix water problems. That was it. But life has a way of shaping us in unexpected ways.

Every busted pipe, every toxic job site, every late night at the club… they all served as training grounds. All the pain, my heart stopping, the fear in my family's eyes, the helplessness I once felt became the fuel I needed to create something that could help others heal.

I used to think clean water was the goal. Now I know *clean* is just the starting point. Real water, the kind your body recognizes, absorbs, and thrives on, goes beyond filtration. It's about energy, charge, and nourishment. And it has the power to change lives.

Mine included.

This journey has taken me from dirty basements to skyscrapers and even high-level medical conferences... from fixing broken plumbing to building systems that doctors recommend.[6] And the best part is, I didn't do it alone. My wife stood by me. My kids inspired me. My team believed in me. And the clients we serve every day remind me why I keep going.

I've said it before, and I'll say it again: I trained my whole life for this moment.

And I'm just getting started.

* The ideas and information shared here are not medical advice—please check with your healthcare provider before making changes to your healthcare routine

---

[6] **pH Prescription LLC**
www.phprescription.com

Chapter 21:
The Day the Sun Set

You are my sunshine, my only sunshine…

In 2013, the wheel of life turned again, and this time, it broke me. My father passed away suddenly, and even now, those words don't feel real. His death came like a thief in the night, swift and unforgiving, stealing the man who had always been my anchor.

The cause? A lifetime of toxic exposure. Decades spent working around asbestos as a plumber and pipefitter. Years of breathing in poisons no one warned him about. And near the end, it was the medications, the ones meant to help, that added weight to an already burdened body. It was a cruel echo of how my grandfather died from mesothelioma, buried deep in the lungs, silent but relentless.

That day started like any other. I was meeting with a client, talking about water systems and business as usual. My phone kept buzzing. I ignored it at first. But then something deep in my gut told me to pick up.

The next call was LeAnn. Her voice cracked with panic and grief.

"Get to the hospital. It's your dad… it's bad." Everything in me went still.

Normally, I would've been an hour away from my parents' house. But not that day. That day, I was ten minutes down the road from the hospital. I don't believe in coincidences anymore. I believe I was exactly where I was meant to be.

I drove like a man possessed, my heart pounding, hands clenched on the wheel. When I reached the ER, a nurse stopped me at the door. She looked at me with the kind of eyes that already know what you don't want to accept.

"I want to prepare you," she said softly. "He's gone." Time cracked wide open.

Inside, my mother stood at his side, stoic and shattered. She turned to me, her face trembling, and collapsed into my arms. "How did you get here so fast?" she asked.

I didn't have an answer. I only held her. She told me I was her rock that day... but truthfully, she had always been mine.

That night, back at their home, the air was thick with grief. The phone rang nonstop. Condolences poured in. Everyone asked how Mom was holding up. I couldn't take it anymore. I stepped outside into the night.

The world was still.

And then, like a sign from somewhere beyond, a melody drifted through the air from a neighbor's yard:
"You are my sunshine, my only sunshine..."

It was my dad's favorite song. And my grandfather's too.

I stood there on the porch, tears streaming down my face, that simple song wrapping around me like a hug from the past. I knew, in that moment, that he wasn't gone. Not really. He was with me. Just... different now.

In the days that followed, the memories flooded in. My father wasn't a man of many words, but his presence was constant. His loyalty unwavering. His strength undeniable. Yet in the silence that followed his passing, another truth came into focus: my mother had been the glue all along.

Her strength. Her resilience. Her sacrifices, so many of them unseen. She held the family together through every storm and never once asked for credit. She didn't need to. Her love was loud enough without a word.

My father gave me my name, my grit, my will to fight. My mother gave me my heart, my compass, my sense of home. **I love you, Mom!**

My Amazing Mother

When a Door Closes...

Just days after my father passed on, it was the weekend of my birthday, and we tried to lift the heaviness. LeAnn organized a small gathering at our home while the family was in town to pay their respects to my father.

Cosmo had heard about my loss and came to that gathering for condolences. Wanting to help in his own way, he told my wife, "If it helps, Leo can take out his old Italian boat for his birthday." It was a kind gesture, one that meant more than he probably knew.

That's when I also decided to take the guys out on the water, chasing some joy through the heartache.

We loaded up the 27-foot Italian boat with me, my brother Steven, Big Jim (my favorite cousin), his son Jimmy, and my brother-in-law Kenny. We hit the throttle hard, racing out to the sandbar, cutting across the water like we were leaving our pain behind. Fast boats have a way of making people smile, at least for a little while.

On the way back, we stopped at Sailor's Return for a drink. Jimmy forgot his ID, so he ended up drinking a soda, or maybe it was milk, depending on who tells the story. We all laughed. It felt good to laugh.

Later that evening, Big Jim and I sat and talked. We reflected on Dad's life, his passing, and how much had changed. Big Jim turned to Jimmy and said, "I bet you wish your Uncle Lee would adopt you and bring you down here. It's paradise."

Without missing a beat, Jimmy said, "If there's ever a spot for me, I'd love to give it a shot."

That moment stopped me. It hit me hard, full circle. Jimmy's dad had worked with my father, and they both had worked with my grandfather, the original trailblazer of plumbing in our family. Three generations. Now here was Jimmy, ready to pick up the torch.

After they returned to New Jersey, Jimmy kept calling and checking in, asking if a spot had opened. I didn't want to rush it. I needed to be sure I could give him full-time work. Taking on someone's future, especially that of a family member, is no small thing. I didn't want to bring him down only for it to fall apart.

But when the timing was right, I brought him on.

He started, like everyone else, installing systems, riding with Leo Jr., and learning the ropes. However, when we expanded into Aquapellis shower systems, I gave Jimmy a challenge: find a way to electronically balance pH and build a waterproof control panel for adding the nutrients.

He came back with something beyond anything I imagined.

Me and Jimmy

Not just a panel, but a full computer. Waterproof, color touchscreen, real-time data, intuitive controls. It was way more than I asked for, but exactly what we needed.

Since then, Jimmy and I have traveled across the country together, building some of the most advanced water systems in the world.[7] When I say there's nothing we can't do, I mean it.

When my father passed, it felt like a door closed forever. Because he passed, Jimmy showed up, and suddenly, a window opened. It's strange how life works like that. These moments seem random, but they're part of something bigger.

Just like when I was born and my grandfather passed away, it's all part of the great, mysterious circle of life.

So, here's to you, Jimmy. For honoring the legacy, for showing up, and for growing with us. I'm proud of the man you've become and the loyalty you've shown. We've got big things ahead. We're just getting started.

Carrying His Light

Losing my dad changed everything. It was sudden. It was brutal. And it left a hole no words can fill.

But in the quiet that followed, I found clarity.

I started to see all the ways I carry him with me. His grit. His strength. His belief in doing the job right. He didn't need to be loud. He just showed up. Every single day. For his work. For his family. For me.

That night on the porch, when the song "You Are My Sunshine" echoed through the darkness, it wasn't just a coincidence. It was a connection. I knew then I'd never hear his voice again, but everything he stood for still lives on. In me. In my mom. In every job I take on, I do so with a purpose.

---

[7] **Aquapellis Shower Systems**
www.aquapellis.com

He taught me that what you build with your hands matters. But how you love your family, that's the real legacy.

Me, front left, Nadine, Dean, and Leo Jr. to the right

My brother Steven once summed it up at one of Dad's birthday parties:

"Dad got a magic toolbox that fixes anything." Steven, you were right. He really did.

And now we carry that toolbox with all its wisdom and wear, and I do my best to use it the way he did: to lift people, to protect them, to fix what's broken.

He was my sunshine.

And now… I shine because of him.

* The ideas and information shared here are not medical advice—please check with your healthcare provider before making changes to your healthcare routine.

Chapter 22:
Healing in Texas

Grateful for Clients who Became Family and Friends

When we lost my father, just a few weeks later I was scheduled to be in Texas, delivering a keynote speech at a major medical conference hosted by Dr. Jerry Tennant. I was prepared to cancel. Grief was overwhelming and hit me hard, and I didn't feel like I had the strength to stand up in front of a crowd and pretend I was okay.

But then I asked myself, ***What would my dad do?***

The answer was clear. He'd go to work. That's what he did every single day. No excuses. No surrender. He never stopped and never gave up. So I had a decision to make. Sit at home and let the pain swallow me whole... or get on that stage and let the pain drive me to do something meaningful.

So, I flew to Texas that Friday. The truth is, I needed the distraction.

By the time I landed, I still felt like I was drifting in the clouds. I didn't know all the people or all the moving parts of the conference, but they welcomed me with open arms. They knew what I had just gone through, and their kindness meant more than I could ever say.

That trip was different. I wasn't my usual talkative self. I gave my lecture quietly and then took a seat like everyone else. I didn't make small talk in the halls. I just sat, listened, and tried to absorb something that might help me heal.

Me and Dr. Tennant

Dr. Tennant was the first to speak, and the metaphor he used stopped me cold.[8]

He said, *"If your car flips over into a ditch, you don't just try to start it up again. You flip it back over. You check the oil. You refill the coolant. You inspect everything before you even think about turning the key."*

It made perfect sense. You don't slap a Band-Aid on a wreck and expect it to run like new. You go system by system, part by part, just like the human body. You repair what's broken. Replenish what's missing. Only then can you turn the key and expect life to get back on track.

And for a guy like me, someone who grew up under the hood, rebuilding muscle cars from the frame up, that analogy lit a fire. I've brought engines back from the dead. I've

---

[8] **Dr. Jerry Tennant, MD – Tennant Institute**
www.tennantinstitute.com

straightened bent frames, cleaned out years of carbon buildup, and rewired tangled messes into roaring machines. I knew the process. I lived it.

So, when Dr. Tennant laid it out like that, something clicked deep inside.

If I could rebuild a car ... I could rebuild myself.

That was the moment I truly believed healing was possible, not just for me, but for anyone walking around with unseen damage, running on fumes, thinking they just needed to push through. No. Some of us need to be flipped upright, refilled, and rewired. Some of us need a full rebuild.

And from that day forward, that's exactly how I approached it.

Water is a great place to start, but it's not the whole picture. It doesn't replace food, minerals, vitamins, movement, or rest. We need all of these to build new, healthy cells. Because once our bodies stop building those, everything starts to fall apart.

Next came Dr. Nathan Bryan, an expert on nitric oxide.[9] His talk on blood flow and cardiovascular health struck a personal chord. I've battled high blood pressure, so I paid close attention. He explained how even using mouthwash can cause high blood pressure by killing the good bacteria in your mouth that help your body produce nitric oxide. No nitric oxide means no proper blood flow. It made perfect sense. I already knew fluoride had triggered issues for me. Why not mouthwash, too?

---

[9] **Dr. Nathan Bryan, PhD – N1O1**
www.n1o1.com

Me And Dr Nathan Bryan[10]

"We became friends right here. That presentation changed the way I looked at health. Dr. Bryan was new to me back then, but from groundbreaking lab discoveries to genuine connections, it's clear he's not just a colleague. He's been a true friend and an ongoing source of inspiration."

Then Dr. Steve Evans, a biological dentist, took the stage. His talk hit me the hardest. He explained how root canals leave dead tissue in your body. And dentistry is the only branch of medicine where you're allowed to leave something dead inside. Those teeth become breeding grounds for bacteria and endotoxins. Your body is tricked into thinking it can heal them, but it never can. The damage spreads silently.

Even more alarming, teeth are connected to your heart, lungs, and other organs through energy meridians. When he

---

[10] **Dr. Nathan Bryan, PhD – N1O1**
www.n1o1.com

mentioned that, I perked up. I'd had a heart attack a year earlier. And I had a mouth full of root canals.

I decided to see him.

At the time, my close friend Lewis was fighting ALS. It's the cruelest disease I've ever seen, slowly stealing your nervous system until you can't even breathe on your own. Lewis and I went in together to see Dr. Evans.[11] He started with Lewis, removing mercury fillings and deeply infected teeth. Over a few visits, we got him all cleaned up.

Dr Steve Evans and I

Then it was my turn. Dr. Evans performed a cone beam scan, reviewed the results, and shook his head. "You've got seven infected root canals," he said. "And a few are on your heart circuit." He recommended someone closer to home just in case, to make it easier on me, but I told him straight: "No. I want *you* to do it."

It took three trips to get them all out. He showed me pictures of each tooth blackened, infected, with abscesses that looked

[11] **Dr. Steve Evans, DDS – Healthier Smiles Dental**
www.healthiersmilesdental.com

like lungs growing out of the roots. Every time he pulled one, I felt a little lighter, clearer.

The last tooth was a lower right canine, root canaled when I was seventeen after a karate kick shattered the root. It had formed what they called a "sterile abscess." When he pulled it, it felt as though the fog in my mind had lifted instantly. I could *think* again.

Dr. Evans saved me from myself. And today, I tell anyone who will listen, I will never get another root canal, not after what I've learned.

In the years since, everyone I met through that Texas conference has become like family. Dr. Tennant and his team. Dr. Evans, his wonderful wife Barbara, and his incredible staff.[12] Dr. Bryan and his network. And everyone at Senergy Medical Group. I'm grateful to all of you.

And then there's Big Bill Bagwell, my Texas brother, helping me on installs, sharing stories, always showing up. These are bonds I'll never forget.

One of the great blessings of those conferences is that they often bring me to Phoenix, where, at the time, my daughter Nadine and one of my sons, Dean, also later moved to. That's where my former wife moved after the divorce. She eventually married a great guy named Ted. He didn't have kids of his own but stepped in like a champ, and I'm truly grateful for the father he's been to our children.

It's funny how life changes. Years ago, I was angry, bitter even. But today we all sit down to dinner like one big family. My current wife and my former wife get along just fine. And Ted and I had some great conversations. We're different in

---

[12] **Dr. Steve Evans, DDS – Healthier Smiles Dental**
www.healthiersmilesdental.com

169

many ways, but we share a bond built on love for the same kids. I'm thankful she found him. Welcome to the family, Ted.

When my dad passed, M, Ted, Dean, and Nadine all flew in for the funeral. It meant the world to me; they all came.

During the Celebration of Life, my brother Steven pointed to the bar where my first girlfriend, my former wife, and my current wife were all standing together. He elbowed me and said, "Lee, jump in there. I'll get a picture."

I didn't. But it was funny. Steven has a way of making you laugh even on a day like this. He may have missed his calling as a stand-up comedian.

As fate would have it, just a few years later, M lost her father. We were in Vegas at another conference when we got the call. I turned to LeAnn and said, "Change of plans, we're driving to Phoenix." We had to be there for him. For her. For our kids. I even had the opportunity to speak at his service. He was always cracking jokes, even when I first met him.

"You look like a nice enough guy," he said. "But what are you doing with *my* daughter?"

I didn't know how to respond.

"Run," he said, dead serious. "Run fast."

When we got divorced, he said, "Told you so."

But in the end, we laughed. And I was proud to stand up and honor him. That day meant something to all of us. It was great to see M's family over the years; they have all remained so kind to me.

See, you never really know how things will turn out. But I do know this: I'm glad I kept showing up.

Even when it was hard. Especially when it was hard.

Looking back, that weekend in Texas was more than just a conference; it was a turning point. I arrived broken, grieving, and unsure if I even belonged there. But in the quiet moments of sitting, listening, and learning, something shifted. I found healing. I found direction.

I had just lost my father, but I carried his spirit with me. Somehow, that gave me the strength to keep going. I delved deeper into understanding the human body, the true nature of healing, and the hidden dangers we live with every day. And through it all, I began to see what really matters: showing up for others, doing the hard work, and keeping your heart open even when it hurts.

Life has a way of bringing things full circle. I'm grateful for the pain, the people, and the purpose that shaped this part of the journey.

I truly don't believe I'd still be here or that this book would even exist without my Texas family. Thank you for being there exactly when I needed you.

* The ideas and information shared here are not medical advice—please check with your healthcare provider before making changes to your healthcare routine.

Chapter 23:
Capfuls of Goodbye

"A healthy person has 1000 wishes, a sick person has 1."

A round this time, we were deep into a new project, one of our biggest. It started in Toronto and Southern California, and everything was moving so fast. A yacht client from Boca Raton had reached out with an idea: to add a high-end water filtration system as a value, to add to their luxury home with a leak detection service. They didn't just want clean water; they wanted something no one else had.

So, we got to work.

We designed a sleek system that makes water feel soft without the need for salt or moving parts, utilizing a vortex that alters the water's bonds to achieve a soft water feel while reducing chlorine and improving water quality. It was beautiful. We named it the **Water Management System,** WMS for short. We later made some changes, and it is now called the 'QuadVortex®.'

We spent months in meetings, from the Toronto boardrooms to Boca yacht lounges. The client wanted thousands of them, and fast. That meant engineering, molding, NSF certification for chlorine removal, proving it was lead-free, and getting it all into production.

It took time. But we passed every test.

Soon, we were installing WMS systems all over Canada and California. My team and I worked day and night, taking pride in what we were building. It felt like momentum. Like purpose. Like the kind of work my dad would've smiled about. And I was finally getting back to myself until the phone rang.

I had just flown home from months in California and landed back in Fort Lauderdale. Dragging my bag to the car, tired but ready to be home, when my phone lit up. It was LeAnn.

Her voice cracked.

"I know this is bad timing... but Lewis is in the hospital in Stuart. He's not doing well."

I stopped right there in the airport parking garage. The echo of footsteps and car horns faded into silence around me. My heart sank. I knew what was coming.

While I was trying to recover my own health, Lewis wasn't as lucky.

ALS had a tight grip on him, and it never let go.

We had been close for decades. Grew up together in New Jersey. He even lived in the same house my family would eventually move into. We shared roots, memories, music, muscle cars, everything. He was like a brother to me.

When I moved to Florida, Lewis eventually followed. He was laser-focused, clean, and determined. No alcohol. No drugs, especially no drugs. He had gotten clean in his early twenties and never looked back. His NA group became his chosen family, and I respected the hell out of that. I even went to meetings with him sometimes, just to support the path he was walking. That was Lewis, strong as hell, and a heart twice as big.

He could fix anything with his hands. Machines. Motors. Life itself, except for the one thing that mattered most. I wish with everything in me we could've fixed him.

Watching ALS take him down was brutal. It stole him slowly, piece by piece. His strength, speech, and dignity. I hated every second of it. I was losing my brother far too soon, and there wasn't a damn thing I could do.

"A healthy person has 1000 wishes, a sick person has 1."

Lewis was supposed to be my best man in Key West. But last-minute family issues kept him in Jersey. I told him we'd get another shot at that speech someday. We never did.

A few years earlier, right after I lost my dad, we found out Lewis had ALS. He fought hard. Stayed healthy. Ate clean. Took care of himself like he still had something to prove. But ALS doesn't care how strong you are. It just strips you down.

The moment I got that call, I drove straight to Stuart. No stops. No sleep. I just had to get there.

By the time I walked into the hospital room, Lewis was already slipping into a coma. His brother was there. A few close friends. I grabbed his hand and told him I was here. Told him I wasn't leaving. His breath was heavy. Labored. His mouth was dry. His tongue cracked from thirst. LeAnn met me there and handed me a bottle of water.

I poured just a capful into his mouth. His lips smacked. Then he smiled.

So I kept going.

We sat through the night, me giving him those little sips, talking to him like we were teenagers again. The guys in the room nodded and said, "If it helps, keep going." So I did. It was the only comfort I had left to give.

Then a doctor walked in and snapped at me. "Stop giving him that. It's agitating him."

I looked him in the eye and asked, "Are you going to save him?"

He looked down. "No."

"Then get out," I said. "I'll let you know when he's gone. Until then, let me take care of my friend."

Nobody argued.

Turns out, I was listed as his number one contact. The one who'd get the call when it was time. And that time came.

A nurse quietly asked if we wanted to give him a final "comfort dose," a shot to help ease his passing. I knew what that meant. I've been around enough doctors to understand their language. Hell, most people think I *am* one. I talk like one. I write like one. I've got a medical symbol on my company logo. At conferences, they call me "Dr. Leo."

My office still laughs when someone says, "Dr. Leo, line one."

But that day... there was nothing funny.

At around 11 a.m., Lewis passed, just like that. The light left the room, and the world lost one of the good ones.

That day broke me.

Losing Lewis, right after losing my father, was like being gutted twice. Two giants in my life have gone back-to-back. It shifted something in me. Made me more committed than ever. But not in some professional, polished way.

In a human way.

Lewis and Me

Because Lewis was more than a friend, he was my brother. And he deserved more time.

Afterward, I didn't go home and rest. I sat in the car with the engine off, hands frozen on the wheel, staring at nothing.

LeAnn just sat with me. No words. No rush. That's true love, when someone just *sits* in your silence and stays.

When I finally walked through the door at home, the kids saw a version of me they'd never seen before. Not just tired. Not just worn out. But shattered. The rock of the family cracked wide open.

I dropped to my knees and cried like a child. I couldn't hold it in. And when my kids saw me like that, raw and broken, they cried too. Not just for Lewis, but for me. Because they knew what he meant to me, they knew what we had all just lost.

But from that heartbreak, something powerful rose.

I saw clearer than ever what my mission really is. It's not just about making water cleaner. It's not just about fancy tanks, certifications, and systems.

It's about comfort. It's about dignity. It's about love.

If a *capful* of water can bring a dying man one last smile, one final moment of peace…

Imagine what a *lifetime* of healthy water can bring to the living.

That's the mission.

That's the legacy. Rest easy, Lewis.

You'll be missed more than words can say. I'll carry you with me always.

* The ideas and information shared here are not medical advice—please check with your healthcare provider before making changes to your healthcare routine.

Chapter 24:
From Basements to Billionaires

I never set out to work with billionaires.
But somehow, that's exactly where I ended up.

Where the Water Takes Us

Penthouse views. Private jets. Mansions with marble floors and mega yachts that cost more than small towns. One day, I was in a high-rise in Manhattan, the next on a dock in Miami, boarding a vessel with more water toys than the average marina. These weren't just millionaires. These were the people who *owned* the buildings with their names on them.

But here's the part that surprised me most: *just about all of them didn't even have water filtration systems in their homes.* Not a single filter. No protection. Nothing but tap.

And so, I changed that.

Not because they were rich. Not because they were famous. But because they were human and just as vulnerable to what flowed from their pipes as the family of four in a modest home. The water didn't care how much money you had. But I did.

At this point in my life, I was traveling everywhere. Keynote speaker at medical and wellness conferences in nearly every major U.S. city: Chicago, LA, Dallas, Atlanta, and New York. I'd step off the stage and someone would approach me. A doctor. A clinic owner. A celebrity's assistant. And the calls would come. "Can you come to the house?" "Can you take a look at our water?" "We've heard what you're doing is different."

And it was.

After my father passed, something in me shifted. I poured myself into my work like never before, not just to build a company, but to build a *solution*. A real answer to the toxic reality we all shared. I went deeper into the science, pushed harder with my team, and we started perfecting systems that didn't just clean water, they restored it.

Because here's what I know now:

You don't have to be a millionaire to deserve clean water.

You just need someone who cares enough to make it possible.

We've built systems for every kind of home: small, large, and even off-grid. And we've worked hard to make them accessible.

Today, I work side by side with my wife, LeAnn. With the kids grown and moved on and no pets left in the house, we've become a true team on the road. We travel together as much as possible, laying out systems, speaking at conferences, and pouring our time into educating others.

Wherever I go, I bring my own water cooler. Every event. Every city. I hand out cups to attendees, vendors, doctors, and even security staff. If you're there, you get water. Hydration is the message, but it's also the mission. People now *look* for me at events, hoping I'll be there to keep them hydrated. It's become a signature.

I'll never forget the WQA conference in Las Vegas, where I was walking around in a state of full-on AFib. I had my meds in hand, but no water. I sat there, medication in my mouth. Hard to find water at a water quality event. I needed water. *My water.* That moment changed everything. Good thing I was there. It lit a fire in me to never show up to a conference again without bringing healing water with me.

These days, the mission is still growing, and so is the family. Both my sons are now fathers. I'm a grandfather several times over, and yes, we even have a **Leo the Sixth** now. Life really does come full circle. The next generation is already here, growing fast, strong, and healthy. Just like the water they drink.

Our business grew fast. So fast, in fact, we had to move offices **three times in ten years** just to keep up with the demand. We started small, but today we have systems for just about every size home and every kind of budget. You don't need to be rich to have clean, healthy water. But it's through working with the rich that I met people who opened more doors than I ever imagined.

We built a team we could trust. My wife LeAnn and my son Leo Jr., my head technical adviser, my nephew Jimmy, and even my daughter Nadine are part of it now, alongside a handful of talented techs and sales personnel. We've also started signing up affiliates across the country with doctors, health spas, wellness clinics, and people who believe in our mission and recommend our systems to their clients. We barely advertise. It's all word of mouth. And it works.

Watching my team create their own stories with me, just like I had with my dad, means more than I can put into words. Jimmy's dad, Big Jim, worked with both my dad and my grandfather in plumbing. We've got stories that go back decades, and they still come up at lunch or dinner after a long day in the field. That's how we operate: we get the job done, good days and bad, and then we break bread together as a family.

We never know where we're heading next. Could be the Bahamas. It could be Mexico. It could be just up the road. One thing's for sure, we go where we're needed.

Road Trips and Jets

After most conferences, we'd pick up enough work in the area to justify staying a while. Sometimes we shipped systems, but if we had a solid list of installs, we'd load up one of the Sprinter vans with equipment and hit the road.

New York. Dallas. LA. I've done them all with Leo Jr., Walker, and Jimmy, or sometimes all. Those trips were bonding time, long drives, long installs, good food, and great conversations.

Clients would often invite us into their homes or out for dinner. Some trips took us through places I used to only dream about, **The Hamptons, Martha's Vineyard, and Nantucket**. I've even had clients fly me in on their private jets for emergency service calls. One of those calls took me to the **Virgin Islands**, where a water maker had gone down on a mega-yacht. The owner wouldn't let anyone else touch it but me.

When I got there, I found **jellyfish clogging the pre-filters**. Reached in, got stung. Nothing a little vinegar couldn't fix. I got it running again and, in the process, spent a few days living on a beautiful yacht, flying first class. Yeah... I've been blessed by my clients more than once.

That sure beats the dirty basements and crawl spaces I once worked in.

Chasing Fast and Free

I've always loved driving cool cars, flying planes, and racing boats, anything that moves fast. I've driven just about every type of vehicle out there. Planes? Yep. Boats? Definitely. I've even driven most heavy equipment, including a bulldozer, which my dad always said was the same as a tank. Still on my bucket list? A tank, a submarine, and a helicopter. One day...

Back to the Sea

Not long ago, I felt the pull to get back on the water. LeAnn and I went to the **Miami Boat Show**, and there she was: a center console combined with a go-fast hull with **"This boat will go 80 MPH"** stamped on the side. It wasn't my usual style, but that line got me. I almost bought it right there.

But Vegas was calling. We had to leave for the A4M anti-aging conference at the Venetian. Great place, great people. But I couldn't stop thinking about that boat. On my iPad, I found three just like it for sale. The first two sold within hours. I put a deposit on the third, sight unseen. I even closed the deal **right there at our booth in Vegas;** the bank sent an agent straight to the conference.

As soon as we got back to Florida, I started planning the trip to get the boat. LeAnn gets anxious on long rides, especially when I'm hauling something big. So, she said, "Take Terry." That's **Tear Bear,** my best friend in Florida. We met way back in '89 and just kept crossing paths. Martial arts, at the gym, and even muscle cars, our kids are the same age, and even our wives share the same birthday. Every year, we celebrate together.

So, I called him. "You wanna take a road trip and go get this boat?" He didn't hesitate. "Let's go."

Twelve hours later, we were in Alabama. It was pouring rain the day we picked it up. The guy selling it worked for Homeland Security, and the boat had been a Coast Guard vessel. Still had the lights and decals. The name?

"KNOT ON DUTY."

That boat ran like a dream. Fastest I've ever had. She lived most of her life in the Gulf, though.

A little too light for the open ocean, we felt like a ping-pong ball in rough water. Still, she brought us back to the water. And that's where I belong.

Legacy in Motion

Looking back, I realized that everything I've built wasn't just about water; it was about people. About family. About movement. I've spent my life chasing flow, whether through pipes, across highways, or out on the open sea. And the thing about flow is it never stands still. Neither do I.

My dad taught me the value of doing things right, putting your name on your work, and standing behind it. I've tried to carry that into everything I do, from the smallest residential installation to the largest mega-yacht water system.

Now, with my family by my side, we've created something that lives beyond just business. It's a mission. It's personal. And it's growing.

We never know where the next call will come from: Texas, Turks and Caicos, or Tennessee. But one thing's for sure:

We go where we're needed.

* The ideas and information shared here are not medical advice—please check with your healthcare provider before making changes to your healthcare routine.

Chapter 25:
When the World Locked Down

Life doesn't ask for permission.
It just happens in a moment, and then it's gone.

I didn't set out to write about so much sadness.
But when you tell the truth, you don't get to pick and choose.
You just say what happened.

This was the hardest part for me to write. No one knew what was coming.

When COVID hit, it wasn't just a virus.
It was a storm; silent, invisible, and it tore through the world without mercy.
Fear moved faster than any sickness. Confusion followed.
Chaos wasn't far behind.

We sat there, like everyone else, staring at the TV, wondering what tomorrow would even look like.

At the time, LeAnn and I had a trip planned to the Keys.
The hotel called and said they were still open, so we decided to go.
We packed fast, threw our bags in the car, and hit the road, not sure if we were running toward something or away from it.

We didn't know if we could eat in a restaurant. We didn't know if the beaches would be open. All we knew was that we needed to feel alive.

When we walked into one of our favorite places, we half expected to find it abandoned.
Instead, the place was alive.
The bar was full. Every table was taken.

The laughter, the music was there. It was like stepping into a different world.

I asked the waitress what the rules were.
She smiled and said, **"You're in the Keys. No rules. Enjoy."**

I will never forget that moment.
It made me proud to live in Florida.
Proud that at least somewhere, people still believed in freedom of living, even in the face of fear.

But when we got home, the world we left behind was still waiting for us.
Empty streets. Closed businesses.
Airports that looked like war zones.
Clients were terrified to let anyone near their homes.

We shut down the office for a while out of respect, out of fear, maybe both.
But the calls kept coming. And then they got louder.

People needed water.
Not just clean water, safe water.
They needed something they could trust when everything else felt like it was falling apart.
They were trapped at home now, cooking, cleaning, drinking tap water they never trusted, and they were scared.

So, we came back.
We answered every phone call. We packed every filter by hand.
We showed up, even when it felt like the whole world wanted to hide.

There was no guarantee we were safe. There were no answers.
Only the questions that kept playing on a loop in the back of my mind:

187

What's really going on? Are we all in danger? Are we going to make it through this?

We just kept moving forward. One day at a time. Because sometimes, that's all you can do.

A Day on the Water
With the roads empty and the world closed tight, we decided to escape the only way we knew how by boat. LeAnn, Junior, and I loaded up and pointed the bow south toward Palm Beach.

The water was wide open.
No yachts. No jet skis. No one. Just silence and sky.

It felt like we were the last three people left on Earth.

When we got to Jupiter, I pulled into Burt Reynolds Park. I beached the bow of the boat, unpacked some sandwiches, and we let the afternoon settle in around us.

The sun on our faces.

The ripple of the water against the hull.
For the first time in weeks, maybe months, it felt like life could still be simple.

Then, within minutes, the marine patrol pulled up alongside us.
The officer gave a quick glance at the Homeland decals and the Coast Guard registration on my boat.
He stood a little straighter, offered a respectful salute, and said, "Sir, all parks are closed due to the pandemic. Please move three feet offshore and drop anchor, enjoy your day, Sir."

Three feet. That's all they asked.
The world was falling apart, but here, three feet was the difference between shutdown and freedom.

He thought I was with Homeland Security.
I could see it in his face, the way he spoke, the way he held himself.
Maybe it was the look of the boat. Maybe it was the name painted across the boat:
KNOT ON DUTY.

It added to the mystique. I smiled and told LeAnn,
"I'm never changing that name."

And in that moment, anchored just outside the rules, I felt like myself again.
I wasn't trapped in fear; I wasn't locked behind a screen or a closed door.
Out there, on that open water, I could still breathe. I could still be free.

Water Saved Me Again

Two years into the madness, after all the fear, all the headlines, all the arguments, COVID finally caught up with us.

LeAnn and I got it at the same time.
It hit us hard, like a bad cold you couldn't shake. But it never got worse than that.
And I believe the reason why was simple: water.

Not just any water, the pure, living water we had created for ourselves.

Our chlorine-free pool was infused with pure oxygen and ozone.
Every day, we soaked in it for hours. We let the oxygen fill our lungs.
We let the water pull the fear, the sickness, the heaviness out of our bodies.

While the world stayed locked inside, suffocating in fear and isolation, we found our cure in the one thing that had always been there for me: water.

It saved me once when my body was broken. It saved me again when the world broke around me.

But just when it felt like the world was finally opening again, when the air seemed a little lighter, and hope began to creep back in, my world closed forever.

Sister Cindy

My sister, Cindy, was more than just my sibling; she was my first best friend. Four years older than me, she was the calm to my storm. The gentle heart to my wild spirit.

Growing up, she never got into trouble. I, on the other hand, was a handful. My mom used to call me the Energizer Bunny, nonstop energy, all gas, no brakes. But Cindy? She was composed, thoughtful, and kind. The kind of kid every parent dreams about.

I followed her everywhere. She didn't always want me tagging along, but I didn't care. She was my whole world.

Our neighborhood was small, full of girls and not many boys my age. So, Cindy became my companion, even if by default. I had a childhood crush on a few of her friends, and they teased me in good fun. Cindy would roll her eyes, but I knew she loved me anyway.

Her room used to be filled with Billy Joel every night. Even now, decades later, I hear those songs and feel like I'm back in that house, just outside her door.

She was always there. Always helping. Always loving.

Me with my sister Cindy and my brother Steven

A Fragile Fighter

What most people didn't know was how much she suffered behind the scenes. Cindy had **Ehlers-Danlos Syndrome, Type IV**, the most dangerous form. Her body was paper-thin; bruising, tearing, and bleeding without warning.

She was so delicate that even a simple fall could kill her. She was in and out of hospitals throughout her life. She couldn't work long hours on her feet. She had to be cautious at every step.

When she was young, my parents thought I was roughhousing with her, and she'd show up with bruises, and they blamed me. But I wasn't touching her. It was the disease. She was just that fragile.

Despite it all, she lived with grace. With heart. With the kind of courage you can't teach.

She later married and had a beautiful daughter. And in 2020, she remarried. I had the honor of walking her down the aisle this time, like our father had done before.

We were on the beach in Stone Harbor, New Jersey. My mom walked on one side, I on the other. Cindy was glowing. She was happy.

But the world was still in chaos.

The Jab: My Line in the Sand

I'm standing by the river again, watching the bodies float by. Sun Tzu said to be patient and wait by the river long enough, and you'll see the bodies of your enemies drift past.

But the truth is, what I see floating now... they're not enemies. They're friends. Family. People I knew. People I loved. Taken too soon; blood clots, strokes, sudden cancers, *all after the Jab.*

That's what eats at me. That's where the pain lives. These weren't statistics on the news. These were phone calls. Hospital visits. Funerals. These were *real people* whose lives were destroyed by something they never should've been forced to take.

And I'm still here. Still standing on this riverbank. Still waiting for the real criminals, the ones who pushed this poison, who lied, who silenced the truth to come floating by. And they will. I believe that with every cell in my body.

I'm not afraid to speak this truth, no matter who it offends. Because I've *seen* the damage, I've *felt* the grief. I've buried too many to stay silent.

I stand here with pain in my heart and fire in my gut. And I will keep standing. Because one day, justice will come floating by on this river.

And I'll be ready.

The Price of Pressure

My sister's husband, a teacher, was forced to get the COVID vaccine. And even though Cindy didn't want to, she got it too. It was simply pure pressure. She didn't tell me. I found out later from my mom because Cindy didn't want me to be upset. Let me explain.

Not long after, she had a stroke. A clot in her neck dropped her to the floor. She passed out in the laundry room and later woke up, calling her husband.

They rushed her to the hospital. The plan was to run a catheter up through her femoral artery to reach the clot. A high-risk procedure. One that, with her condition, should never have been attempted by just any doctor.

My mom and I drove for hours to see her. COVID rules allowed just twenty minutes each.

When I asked her if she got the shot, she looked me in the eye and said no.

She lied to protect her husband from me.

The Last Goodbye

The hospital said they could handle it. They were wrong.

They tore her femoral artery before they even reached the clot.

She almost died on the table.

She stabilized for a while, but she looked broken, tubes everywhere, her body purple with bruises, her spirit fading. She asked our mom, "Am I going to die?"

What do you say to that?

Days later, while LeAnn was in surgery across the state, my phone rang. It was my mom.

She was sobbing. "We lost her."

I froze. Couldn't breathe. Couldn't speak. I just sat in my truck, parked in a hospital lot, stunned and shattered.

LeAnn was still under anesthesia. I couldn't fall apart. I had to wait.

Hours later, when she finally woke, the first words out of her mouth were, *"How's Cindy?"*

She didn't know. But somehow, she knew.

I told her everything was okay. I had to. I couldn't burden her yet.

Later that night, after a call from my cousin Jimmy, I broke. I cried in front of LeAnn. She knew something was wrong. And finally, I told her:
Cindy's gone.

Her eyes welled with tears. She was devastated. Cindy was like her own sister.

I didn't want to tell her that day. But the pain was too much to hide.

I had grown up learning to hold things in. To be tough. But this broke me.

The Fight for Justice

I reached out to attorneys. One of them, a specialist in medical malpractice, reviewed the case and told me the truth: the hospital had no business touching my sister. They weren't qualified for someone with EDS.

But they were protected. Sovereign. Government-owned. Immune to real lawsuits. We couldn't sue for more than

$200,000, and the legal fees alone would eat that up. Cindy's life was reduced to a technicality.

We could go after the doctors, but it wouldn't bring her back. And the system? It never cared about people like her.

I wanted justice. I still do. But I just want her back.

She left behind a daughter, a grandson she adored, and another granddaughter she never got to meet. She was robbed of her future. They robbed her of her light.

The Truth Hurts

Her death wasn't just about one thing. It was everything.

A rare disease. A rushed vaccine. A careless hospital. And a system that prioritizes immunity over accountability.

They told us the **Jab** would save us. That we wouldn't get **COVID** if we got it. That it was safe.

They lied

And now my sister is gone.

She took care of herself. She lived with caution. But when the world went mad, she followed the rules, and it cost her everything.

Dearest sister Cindy,

You held my hand before I could walk, taught me to listen before I could talk.

A sister, a shadow, a light in the hall
The one I looked up to through it all.

Your laugh, your music, your gentle grace,
Still echo through time, still fill up this place.
You lived with a strength the world couldn't see,
But I saw it all, you gave it to me.

And though this goodbye wasn't fair, it wasn't planned,
I still feel your touch, still feel your hand. So I'll carry your name, your fire, your way, in my heart, every night, every day.
And I'll never stop telling your story until we meet again.

Love always,
Your little brother, Lee

* The ideas and information shared here are not medical advice—please check with your healthcare provider before making changes to your healthcare routine.

Chapter 26:
The Future of Water Technology

Bathing in Power, Not Poison

This all started with a hardheaded plumber from New Jersey, someone more familiar with busted pipes and blowtorches than biological breakthroughs. I wasn't chasing fame or fortune. I was chasing relief. I was searching for answers in a world full of toxins, and I stumbled, by sheer grit and relentless curiosity, into something that felt impossible... until it wasn't.

I don't come from a lab coat background. I come from calloused hands, long days, and a no-nonsense attitude that doesn't buy into hype. But what **we** found is beyond hype. It's real. And it changed everything.

What I Discovered in the Dark

Life has a way of testing you:
Losing loved ones.
Facing your own mortality.
Watching your dreams slip through your hands.

I wasn't trying to be a health guru or inventor. I was just trying to survive. But from those darkest moments, **something extraordinary emerged**.

While everything around me was crumbling, I was quietly building something that could help put people back together.

This wasn't found in a textbook or a university lab.
It was forged in the real world through pain and persistence.

What I uncovered wasn't just clean water.
It was something **more**.[13]

I had the idea that if drinking this new type of energetic water was good, bathing in it would be better. And it was so much more than I ever expected.

I can't help but wonder if I'd had this energized bathing system available to my family and friends, would things be different? Would my father still be here? Would Lewis, my best buddy, still be laughing by my side? Would my sister Cindy still have a fighting chance? I'll never know. But the thought haunts me… because maybe, just maybe, it could have changed everything.

The Silent Danger in Your Shower

Here is what I found:

Most people worry about the water they drink. Maybe they install a filter under the sink or buy bottled water. But here's the kicker: they forget what hits their body the most, **the water they bathe in**.

---

[13] **Aquapellis Shower Systems**
www.aquapellis.com

Let me explain something that could change the way you see your shower forever.

It's simple: a ten-minute shower = drinking 8 glasses of the same contaminated tap water. Think about that.

That's not an exaggeration. It's molecular biology.

Your skin isn't armor. It's alive. It breathes. And it absorbs. In fact, if a molecule is under 750 daltons, it can penetrate your skin, and at 150 daltons, it can enter your bloodstream. No liver, no filter, no digestion, *just a straight shot into your blood*.

Now, guess how small a molecule of chlorine is?
35.4 to 70 daltons.

And most volatile organic compounds (VOCs), pesticides, and pharmaceuticals? They're even smaller. Don't even get me started on "forever chemicals" like PFAS and heavy metals.

Every time you take a hot shower in unfiltered tap water, you're not just rinsing off. **You're absorbing.** You're soaking in a chemical cocktail of chlorine, chloramine, VOCs, and PFAS that go straight through your skin.[14]

If your skin could taste, you'd never step into that water again.

You'd demand bottled water to bathe in.
You'd filter your whole house. And most of our clients do.

Did you know that chlorine is a carcinogen and even deemed a pesticide by our own EPA? Its purpose is to kill living organisms. I had found that removing these toxic chemicals

---

[14] **Hydrogen Water Research**
www.molecularhydrogeninstitute.org

from our water protects not only the skin but the whole body inside and out.

Flip the Script: What Happens When Water Heals

Now here's the other side, the part nobody's talking about.

If harmful molecules can penetrate your body through your skin, **so can healing ones**.

Imagine bathing in water that's not just clean, but **energized**.
Water that's **mineral-rich, negatively charged**, and **infused with molecular hydrogen**.
Water that doesn't just rinse you, it **restores you**.

When you bathe in **healthified** water, your body responds on a cellular level. Your skin drinks it in. Your blood receives it. Your cells wake up.

Bathing in healthy, activated water may be up to **10 times more beneficial than drinking it alone**.

Drinking tap water is bad. Bathing in it? Far worse. Drinking healthy water is good. Bathing in it? Even better.

Most people filter their drinking water and forget the rest. But your skin doesn't forget. And neither does your body.

The Feeling of Living Water

This water speaks to the body.
It doesn't just cleanse, it energizes.

Although I'm not a doctor, from the moment I stepped into
that first shower, I knew.
I felt it.

Skin tingling.
Mind clearer.
Body lighter.

And I wasn't the only one.

Moments I cannot forget.

I remember the man from New York, debilitated by vertigo, who walked out of our shower with steady legs again.

A mother who'd been bedridden for weeks found the strength to sit outside and laugh with her son.

A young boy, once ashamed of his skin condition, regained confidence and health. I stood at his wedding years later. His father said, "You gave him his life back."

There was a woman from Fukushima, devastated by radiation and chemotherapy. She sat in one of our showers for nearly two hours. When she finally stood, it was with a new light in her eyes.

A CPA watched his blood sugar normalize; no new medications were needed, just water itself.

These are just some examples of what we've seen. We do not make medical claims.

Others report reduced pain, improved sleep, radiant skin, and sharper minds. Is it magic? No. It's something deeper.

These aren't anecdotes. We believe we're reawakening dormant systems, helping the body remember how to heal.

The Power Beneath the Surface

Water has always meant life, but what we've tapped into elevates that truth.

We've built water systems that don't just filter, they transform. What once cost over $100,000 to build is now being scaled smarter, smaller, and more affordable.

We're bringing this breakthrough into homes, healing centers, clinics, even yachts and penthouses.[15]

This water feels different. Like a soothing electrical current recharging something long forgotten in the body.

A Clinical Breakthrough in Motion

Now, we're taking the next step: clinical validation.

After years of success stories, we are now working with some of the most respected minds to conduct clinical testing, including.

- Dr. Nathan Bryan, PhD[16]
- Dr. Walter Gil, MD[17]
- Dr. Debra DeMarta, MD[18]

This study isn't just science, it's proof. A push to redefine what this type of water can do for human health.

And the source behind it all? That remains a well-kept secret for now.

What we can share is this: our proprietary process recharges the water in a way that makes it biologically active. It

---

[15] **Aquapellis Shower Systems**
www.aquapellis.com
[16] **Dr. Nathan Bryan, PhD – N1O1**
www.n1o1.com
[17] **Dr. Walter Gil, MD – Testimonial**
pH Prescription Testimonial
www.phprescription.com/testimonial/dr-walter-gil-m-d/
[18] **Dr. Deborah DeMarta, MD**
www.drdeborahdemarta.com

delivers what the body's been craving. It doesn't just cleanse, it activates.

The Science in Motion

These aren't flukes or fairy tales.
This is **biology**.
We believe this water helps the body **remember how to heal itself**.

Our proprietary process recharges water.
It delivers what the body craves.
It doesn't just hydrate, it **activates**.

If I hadn't used it myself, I wouldn't believe a word of it.

One Drop at a Time

There's something poetic about it.

We are putting to use the once-taken-for-granted water molecule. We can now supercharge it to help people **wake up** physically, emotionally, and spiritually.

Artists say it sparks creativity.
Athletes say it boosts stamina.
Parents say it gives them peace.

I've seen the skeptics light up after a single shower.

You can't fake that.

And we've only just begun.

---

* The ideas and information shared here are not medical advice—please check with your healthcare provider before making changes to your healthcare routine.

Closing Thoughts

If you've been with me this far, thank you. This book was extremely challenging for me, a dyslexic, to write.

I will say it again.

I didn't write this book because I wanted to.

I wrote it because I had to.

When you walk through storms that nearly drown you, you start searching for lifelines.

Mine was water.

Not just any water, something deeper.

This discovery isn't the end of my story; it's a new

beginning.

For all of us.

Dr. Alexis Carrel said it best:

"The cell is immortal. It is merely the fluid in which it floats that degenerates. Renew this fluid at regular intervals, give the cells what they require for nutrition, and as far as we know, the pulsation of life can go on forever."

I know this to be true because I live it.

This water nourishes the body from the outside in through the skin, reviving cells and replenishing energy.

And remember: **Healing flows where hope is poured.**

The Future of Water is already here.

And we're just getting started.

Sincerely,
Leo G. Szymborski IV

References & Credibility

The following references were carefully selected to support the research, science, and personal experiences shared throughout this book. They represent respected institutions, medical experts, and companies leading innovation in water science, wellness, and clinical practice.

- **Hydrogen Water Research**
  www.molecularhydrogeninstitute.org
  Referenced on Pages 131, 132, 133, 199
  The Molecular Hydrogen Institute is a global leader in compiling and advancing peer-reviewed studies on the therapeutic benefits of molecular hydrogen. With over 3,000 scientific publications and 200+ clinical trials, their work validates hydrogen's potential in supporting health across multiple organ systems.

- **pH Prescription LLC**
  www.phprescription.com
  Referenced on Pages 149, 151, 152, 154
  A company I founded, specializing in advanced water purification and remineralization systems. pH Prescription's work is recognized nationwide for integrating natural filtration media, hydrogen infusion, and doctor-recommended wellness systems.

- **Aquapellis Shower Systems**
  www.aquapellis.com
  Referenced on Pages 161
  Developer of innovative hydrogen-infused shower technology designed to improve skin health, hydration, and overall wellness.

- **Dr. Jerry Tennant, MD** – Tennant Institute
  www.tennantinstitute.com
  Referenced on Pages 129, 151, 152, 164, 165
  A pioneering physician, integrative medicine leader, and author of *Healing is Voltage*. Dr. Tennant's

research bridges the connection between cellular voltage, water, and human healing.

- **Dr. Nathan Bryan, PhD** – N1O1
www.n1o1.com
Referenced on Pages 166, 167, 203
An internationally recognized scientist in nitric oxide research, with groundbreaking contributions to cardiovascular and metabolic health. And author of several books including. The Secret of Nitric Oxide – Functional Nitric Oxide Nutrition.
- **Dr. Steve Evans, DDS** – Healthier Smiles Dental
www.healthiersmilesdental.com
Referenced on Pages 167, 168, 183
A practicing dentist and advocate for oral-systemic health who integrates advanced water wellness practices into patient care.
- **Dr. Deborah DeMarta, MD**
drdeborahdemarta.com
Referenced on Page 203
A board-certified physician specializing in functional and integrative medicine, known for her expertise in gastrointestinal health and nutrition.
- **Dr. Walter Gil, MD** – Testimonial
pH Prescription Testimonial
www.phprescription.com/testimonial/dr-walter-gil-m-d/
Referenced on Page 203
A respected medical doctor providing direct testimonial evidence of health benefits experienced through pH Prescription water systems.
- **Senergy Wellness**—Resource
www.senergy.us
Referenced on Page 169
Long-time supporter of pH Prescription offering breakthrough healing technologies that are revolutionizing how to approach wellness and alleviate chronic issues.

www.ingramcontent.com/pod-product-compliance
Lightning Source LLC
Chambersburg PA
CBHW051145120626
46547CB00012B/955